Write to the Point!

Principles of Essay Writing

William P. Morgan

Cedar Falls High School
Cedar Falls, Iowa

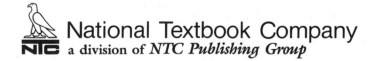
National Textbook Company
a division of *NTC Publishing Group*

To my wife, Sharlene
To my children, Kelli and Joe
To my parents, Helen and Joe
To my colleagues at Cedar Falls High School
To my students who shared their writing,
Thank you.

Drawings by Ruta Daugavietis

Published by National Textbook Company, a division of NTC Publishing Group.
© 1991 by NTC Publishing Group, 4255 West Touhy Avenue,
Lincolnwood (Chicago), Illinois 60646-1975 U.S.A.
Library of Congress Catalog Card Number: 90-60409
Manufactured in the United States of America.

0 1 2 3 4 5 6 7 8 9 RD 9 8 7 6 5 4 3 2 1

Contents

You can't wait for inspiration.
You have to go after it with a club.

—Jack London

Introduction

This is a book about writing, mainly about the kind of writing you do in school. It contains advice and timesaving strategies for making your writing clearer, more interesting, and easier for you to put together.

You should know at the outset, however, that learning to write well is not a passive activity, something that someone does for you, like a dentist filling a tooth. To learn to write well, you have to be involved in the process and you have to be alert to opportunities.

Most professional writers keep a journal in which they store promising ideas, feelings, scraps of information—opportunities. Every so often they pull out the journal, look over what's there, and use the best entries as seeds for their writing.

Take a tip from the pros. Set up a journal or notebook of your own. You may have no use now for that great quote you heard yesterday, but tomorrow or sometime soon, it may be just what you need. So write it down in your journal. Think of your journal as a savings program for the mind. Save a little every day and pretty soon you'll have something to draw on when you're trying to come up with ideas for an assignment.

Besides creating a storehouse of ideas, keeping a journal also helps you maintain the writing habit and gives you a lot of informal practice in pulling ideas out of your mind and putting them on paper. You don't need to worry about sentence structure, spelling, or even complete thoughts—although the journal may be a good place to wrestle mentally with topics that are important to you. On the other hand, parts of your journal may be no more than short notes to yourself.

Your journal will be a lot of things, but you can probably count on its containing a record of what's going on in and around your life. Be certain of one fact—it will be unique, like no one else's.

The following directions will help you set up the journal that works best for you. If you have additional ideas to personalize it, feel free to experiment.

Setting Up Your Journal

1. Buy a spiral notebook about 10½ by 8 inches. Don't try to use your class notebook. You need a place that can be used for journal entries and nothing else. You might consider a three-ring binder so that you can remove material that's of a purely personal nature.

2. Make regular entries, and lots of them. Take ten to fifteen minutes each day to write in your journal. Perhaps your teacher will allow some class time once in a while. If not, make your own time.

3. Anything you feel like writing is fair. There is no such thing as an incorrect journal entry. This is a place to save ideas that can be used later.

4. Date each entry.

5. Label each entry for later identification.

6. Try to write long entries. It encourages you to be more open and worry less about usage rules and spelling.

7. Quantity is very important in journal writing. The more writing you have, the better the chance that a few gems will pop up.

8. This is a good place to use a special writing instrument. Reserving your favorite pen for the journal seems to bring out the best in your creativity.

9. Index your entries every month or so by making a table of contents for the most important ones. Include page numbers.

Getting Started

Keeping a journal may be a very natural thing to do, but the writing doesn't just happen for everyone. Some people can start writing on command. If you are one of those, be grateful. If you are not, the results are worth a little effort, and there is help available. Any time you have trouble getting started, try one of these ideas to get your ballpoint rolling.

1. A popular game to spark the imagination is to make up a list of famous people you would like to invite to a party. You can select people from any time in history, and they need not have lived at the same time. Who are some famous people you would like to invite to your party? What would they think of each other? What questions would you ask them? Include some dialogue.

2. What have you read lately? Include some of your reactions to books, magazine articles, newspaper stories, cartoons, even advertisements.

3. Where do you think you will be ten or twenty years from now? What will you be doing? Will you be married? Have children? What education will you have, and what will your occupation be?

4. Include notes to yourself about jobs you need to do and jobs you hate to do.

5. Think of some experience that gave you a strong emotional reaction and write about it.

6. What television shows have you seen recently that were especially good? Bad? Tell about them.

7. What would happen if you, for some reason, couldn't continue with your present career plans? What might you choose as a backup plan?

8. Have you ever gone people watching? Who are some of the most interesting people you have ever seen? What's the strangest hairdo you've ever seen? Describe unusual clothing you've seen.

9. What advertisements or commercials really bother you? What exactly is so irritating about them? Do you especially admire any current advertisement? Why?

10. Write a letter to someone you don't really know but would like to congratulate for a job well done. This could be a writer, a public figure, or just someone you think might enjoy hearing from a stranger.

11. Make a list of places you wish you had never visited, people you wish you had never met, and books you wish you had never read.

12. Have you ever lost something permanently? Where do you suppose it is at this very moment?

13. Start a collection of quotations you like. Respond to them when the mood strikes you. Here are a few you may like to get you started.

Always grab the reader by the throat in the first paragraph, sink your thumbs into his windpipe in the second, and hold him against the wall until the tag line.

—Paul O'Neil

Facts and truth really don't have much to do with each other.

—William Faulkner

The art of writing is the art of applying the seat of the pants to the seat of the chair.

—Mary Heaton Vorse

I see only one rule: to be clear. If I am not clear, then my entire world crumbles into nothing.

—Stendhal

To write simply is as difficult as to be good.

—W. Somerset Maugham

Fortunately both my wife and my mother-in-law seem to love digging up mistakes in spelling, punctuation, etc. I can hear them in the next room laughing at me.

—Sherwood Anderson

Start collecting quotations in a special section of your journal, and save them for later response. The topic does not have to be writing, and you can say as much or as little as you like about them.

Add a little bit to your journal each day and you'll never be caught without an idea for your next writing assignment.

Beginning in Chapter 3, you will be given regular journal assignments. Some of them will even be fun. But remember, the point of keeping a journal is to accumulate. Then you will never have to face a blank sheet of paper empty-handed or empty-minded.

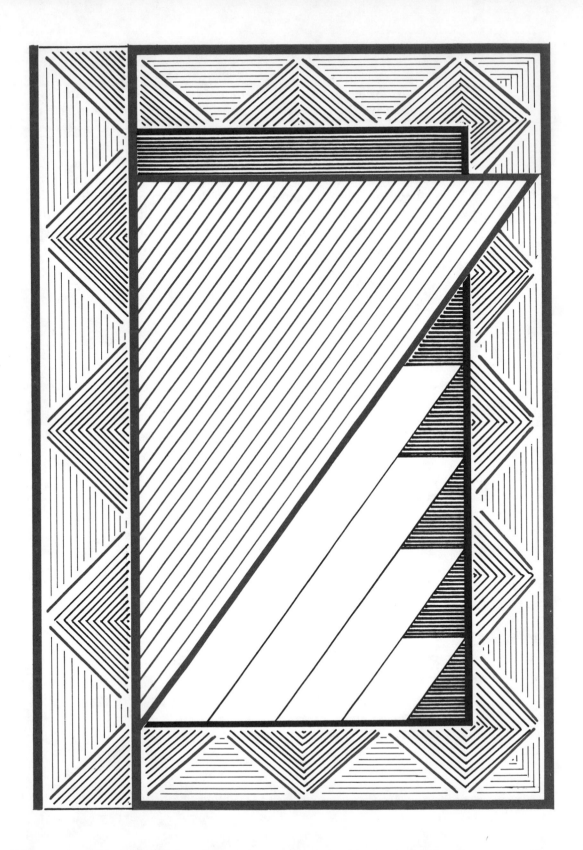

The Persuasive Edge

> *I always remember an epitaph which is in the cemetery at Tombstone, Arizona. It says: "Here lies Jack Williams. He done his damnedest." I think that is the greatest epitaph a man can have—when he gives everything that is in him to do the job he has before him. That is all you can ask of him and that is what I have tried to do.*
>
> *—Harry S Truman*

Don't Be Afraid of Grammar

President Harry Truman went through life as one of the world's most creative spellers. The spelling rules seemed made for someone else, and he never did remember the one about *i* before *e*. Early letters to his wife, Bess, included so many simple errors that eventually he forced himself to keep a spelling dictionary close by. That didn't help with surnames, though, and he became notorious for dreaming up new ways to spell names, even politically important ones.

According to Robert Farrell, who wrote and edited several books about Truman, the President couldn't even master spelling the name of Dean Acheson, his Secretary of State. He knew it wasn't the "Atchison, Topeka, and the Santa Fe," but, just the same, it usually came out "Atchison."

Cities and states caused problems too, but Truman's clear, direct, forceful writing offset the errors. His desire to continue the battle, combined with liberal use of that spelling dictionary, kept the weakness from harming his political career. Today, with Truman listed among the greatest U.S. Presidents, it's safe to say spelling never developed into an insurmountable problem. Mistakes happened. But when they happened, he made the best of them and got on with the real job—dealing with the country's problems.

Don't misunderstand. Correctness does count, and ideally every writer should be a usage expert. Realistically, however, most concern about proper English usage revolves around the impression you make on your reader. It is not a problem of clarity of thought or meaning. Uncertainty about the mechanics of language shouldn't keep you from writing well.

If your desire for success is strong enough to bring you to this book, you probably should consider yourself average or above average in basic skills. As a speaker of American English, you already know the system of our language, the way individual words are put together to form sentences and communicate thoughts. If you doubt your grammatical expertise, read these sentences:

1. John paid the manager five dollars for the broken dish.
2. John five dollars the manager for the broken dish paid.
3. The party is scheduled for this Friday.
4. The party are scheduled for this Friday.
5. My classmates all have seventeen toes.
6. My mother is a doorknob.

Immediately you realized that sentences 1 and 3 represent normal use of the English language. Just as quickly, you saw that 2 and 4 each have a problem. Finally, you recognized that numbers 5 and 6 look like normal English even though they are ridiculous statements.

Most of your problems with English are not really grammatical problems.

You know how to put the words together. If you have any trouble with the language, it is similar to the trouble Truman had. You know when a sentence looks like good English, but you still misspell a lot of the words. Or you may not remember when a comma is needed, a plural pronoun called for, or a colon appropriate. If the nitty-gritty mechanics are your stumbling block, you can get help. Several easy steps can make you a better writer.

1. *Buy an inexpensive spelling dictionary. The Word Book,* based on the *American Heritage Dictionary,* is a great one, and so is the *Instant Spelling Dictionary,* published by Career Institute of Little Falls, New Jersey. It's a matter of personal choice, and you can scout around until you find one that looks good to you. Every bookstore has three or four versions, each a handy 4-by-5-inch book that contains the correct spelling for about 40,000 words. Usually, there will be room in the back to add several dozen of your personal troublemakers. Buy one, keep it handy, and use it.

A useful companion to the spelling dictionary is *The Elements of Style,* by William Strunk, Jr., and E. B. White. Affectionately known among writers as "the little book," this gem is packed with information. It contains basic rules of usage, principles of composition, and suggestions on style. The writer with sense enough to use it as well as the writer's manual in the back of this book will save hours of searching.

2. *Develop a list of free proofreaders.* Ask your mother, father, brother, sister, friend, or classmate to read your work. You will soon find out who is reliable and who isn't. Choose somebody who isn't afraid to tell you what's wrong, and exchange favors if necessary. Someone else can see weaknesses you will never discover. The person who comes to your writing with a fresh eye can help immeasurably.

3. *Say things as clearly as possible.* Don't waste time stewing about a situation you cannot change. Assume you have a certain level of ability in using the language. If you can raise that level, good for you. If quick, significant improvement is unrealistic, just be sure you say things clearly. This means if there is only one way your writing can be interpreted, don't worry about it. Do everything you can to improve your abilities, but don't refuse to write because of uncertainty. The purpose of writing is communication, and if you deliver the message clearly, you have accomplished that purpose.

In the meantime, don't be a quitter. President Truman would have found writing a lot easier if he didn't have to worry about spelling and punctuation, but uncertainty didn't keep him from writing well. I don't think anyone ever accused Harry Truman of being difficult to understand. By the same token, uncertainty about spelling and punctuation shouldn't keep you from writing well.

SUMMARY

1. Uncertainty about the mechanics of language shouldn't keep you from writing well.
2. Use a good spelling dictionary and usage guide.
3. Develop a list of reliable proofreaders.
4. Word your writing as clearly as possible.

DISCUSS

1. To what degree is correctness important in your writing? Explain.
2. What steps can you take to improve your English usage skills?
3. What is the main purpose of writing? How are clarity and correctness related to this purpose?

ACT

1. Answer each of the following questions with a minimum of fifty words. Explain any general statements.
   a. Describe your reading habits. Include novels, newspapers, magazines, nonfiction, comic books, cereal boxes—anything you read.
   b. Describe your knowledge of, or interest in, newsworthy issues of the day.
   c. How do you spend your time when you're not involved in school activities?
   d. Describe your study habits. How much time do you spend studying? Where do you study?
   e. What are your career interests after high school? What further education is necessary? Name two ways in which writing will be important to you.
   f. What are your writing strengths?
   g. What are your writing weaknesses?
   h. What do you hope to gain from this book?
2. Look through some old schoolwork and find something you wrote a year or two ago. How would you improve the writing if you were to do it today? Rewrite it and staple both versions together.
3. Talk to several friends and family members and make a list of four or five people who will agree to proofread your work occasionally.

Make Plans

Good writing is the result of clear thinking, and clear thinking is much easier if you are not bothered by distractions. One way to avoid maddening interruptions is to be sure you have all your tools ready to use. That includes the obvious pencils, pens, and paper, but several other basic tools as well. Don't forget a good dictionary, a thesaurus, and the real timesaver, your spelling dictionary. Along with these, include any research notes you may have taken in preparation for the writing assignment.

Once you are physically organized for writing, you can ease into the mental preparation. Nobody ever says this out loud, but before you can write anything of consequence, you need to take some time to think. Sit down, stare at the wall a while, and consider the problem.

Many textbooks present the writing process as a staccato, unwavering series of steps—1-2-3-4—research, outline, first draft, second draft . . . and chances are you've been trying to do it that way for a long time. Good writing, however, doesn't always work itself out as easily as the textbooks say. Writing is one of those activities where a little time for cool reflection can ease the load tremendously.

To begin, take time to think about the audience you are writing for. Who is going to be reading your work, and what is that person like? Your audience is probably one of your teachers. If this is the case, you are lucky because you know a little about that person. What does Ms. Zapata expect? How would she do the assignment? Even if you can't answer directly for her, it helps to keep her in mind throughout the writing process because you need to know how she visualizes the assignment.

After the audience has been considered, think briefly about your own purpose in doing this assignment. Not "I want to get an A on this paper" but "What do I want the paper to accomplish?" You might decide, "I want to convince Ms. Zapata that the movie *Potemkin* is an outstanding example of early filmmaking." For another class you might try "Alcoholism victimizes the family, too," or "Suicide damages the surviving family members more than most people suspect." Whatever fits the assignment is acceptable, but you must decide early just *what* you want to accomplish.

As soon as you know your purpose and have jotted it down, it's time for a brainstorming session. Think about what information might accomplish your stated goal. Start gathering facts and listing ideas. At this point, order, relative importance, and persuasiveness are not as important as getting ideas down on paper, and the ideas will flow if you ask yourself the right questions—*how, why,* and *when* are almost magical.

Write the ideas down as quickly as you think of them, and don't pause to judge which ones are useful and which are not:

How do surviving family members suffer after a father, brother, sister, or mother commits suicide? List as many ways as you can think of. *Why* do they suffer? *When* do they feel the most pain? In the first few days? After a few weeks? What kinds of emotions do they experience? Jot it all down in a list. Make two or three lists if you want to. Answers to all these questions will give you ammunition when you want to prove that "Suicide damages family members more than most people think."

How do surviving family members suffer?

Mentally:
—guilt   May feel relief in some ways.
            Might even feel anger at person who died.

            imagined vs real
                Could I have prevented it?
                Should I have recognized symptoms?

— Emotions keep changing
— Father/mother guilt as parents?
— Children guilt from unthinking demands?

Physically:
— Immediate shock can make survivor sick.
— Parent could leave economic needs.

Delayed:?   after friends leave.
             Months later find possessions
             Alone at night to wake to mind racing
             with thoughts of person who died.

Physical: — none?

Once you have jotted down some answers to such questions as *how, when,* and *why,* look over your collection of ideas to select the best. Drop the weakest and cluster the others into the most effective natural groups. Cross out any repeats. Do you see any natural categories, or ideas that logically belong together? For example, the guilt a father feels and the guilt a brother feels after a family member's suicide may not be exactly the same, but they should probably be discussed in the same part of your essay.

Arrange these ideas so you can see if a method of organization comes to mind.

How do surviving family members suffer after a father, brother, sister, or mother commits suicide?

How: Guilt — might actually feel relief
Mental suffering
Physical
Shifting emotions — anger, sorrow
Left over economic problems.

Why: Real or imagined guilt.
Could have been prevented?
Were they responsible?
Mother/father failed as parents?
Son/daughter feel they made pressure?

When: Immediate shock can be overwhelming.
After friends leave.
Months later when they find possessions
around house.
Alone at night.

At this point, you might decide to focus the essay even more specifically and concentrate on how suicide affects family members mentally.

A good outline of some sort is probably the most important single element of any essay assignment, and this is the ideal time to start thinking about how you'll want to fit things together. What might be the best sequence of ideas? Write out any main points you want to be sure to include and list supporting ideas and facts for each one.

As you approach the actual writing, plan to do it in an order you find comfortable. Assume that you will have an introduction, a body, and a conclusion to every paper you write, but that does not mean these parts must be written in that order. It won't matter to your reader. In fact there is no way he or she can know if you choose to write the introduction after everything else is completed. If you are comfortable writing the conclusion first, nobody will care so long as the finished product is well organized and reflects clear, sensible, organized thinking.

SUMMARY

1. Assemble your tools: Pen or pencil, paper, dictionary, style and usage manual.
2. Picture your reader: Who will read this?
3. Decide on your purpose. What do you want your reader to think after reading your work?
4. Brainstorm information that will accomplish your purpose. How do you know this is true? Why is it true?
5. Select, drop, and cluster ideas. Put your information in the most effective order.
6. Plan to do the actual writing in whatever order feels comfortable. Keep an open mind.

DISCUSS

1. What equipment should you have available in order to avoid interruptions while you are writing?
2. Describe the process called brainstorming. How selective should a person be while brainstorming?
3. What questions might a writer ask to produce ideas about a subject?
4. What is the purpose of selecting, dropping, and clustering the ideas produced by your brainstorming?

ACT !!

1. Make a list of five individuals or even groups for whom you might possibly find yourself writing. Include your teachers, but try to add some audiences for whom you have not yet written.

2. Pick three of the subjects listed below and, in full sentences, state why you might want to write about each of those topics. What might be your purpose?

   a. parents   e. seat belts
   b. drugs   f. violence
   c. grades   g. teachers
   d. athletics   h. feminism

   Example: "I would show that parents need to respect the privacy of their children."

3. Choose one of the purposes you wrote for question 2 and list five facts, ideas, or incidents that show why you feel that way. Ask yourself questions, such as "Why should parents respect the privacy of their children? When should parents respect the privacy of their children? How should they do it?"

4. Look at your list of ideas from question 3. Which ones seem to be related? Group them into categories. If none show any relationship (which is unlikely but possible), what might be a good order in which to put them?

Use a Thesis Sentence

Get ready for the most important piece of advice about your writing. Copy this advice into your notebook, underline it, mark it with a highlighter, put a gold star by it, and then take ninety seconds to memorize it.

Picture every writing assignment as an opportunity to talk your reader into something.

In other words, convince somebody that you're right. Express an opinion about the topic, and then support that opinion with all the facts you can muster.

When you do this, you overcome the two greatest obstacles to getting an essay started. First, you create a specific purpose for writing ("What can I say? I don't know what to write about in this class"). Second, you give the essay an organizational pattern ("Well, where should I start? What do I say first? Is this enough?").

The first step in planning an essay is to write out your point of view—your opinion, your idea—in one complete sentence. The name for that sentence is *thesis.* Your thesis will be the most important sentence of the essay because it is the idea that you are going to prove.

If the teacher in a film history course assigns a paper on the movie *Citizen Kane,* for example, you make your job much easier by turning the topic into an assertion such as:

Citizen Kane represented a giant leap forward in filmmaking technique.

or

Orson Welles proved his brilliance in making *Citizen Kane.*

or

Orson Welles's remarkable sense of camera placement was responsible for much of the emotional power in *Citizen Kane.*

Turning the topic into an opinion creates the need to explain that opinion and produces a real purpose for your writing. An added bonus is the fact that it creates real interest. If your opinion seems like one that might raise a lot of objections, at least you are sure it won't be greeted with yawns.

At the same time, be certain your thesis is supportable. Take a stand, even one that may raise objections, but don't make a fool of yourself by claiming more than you can prove. The following theses, for example, might be awfully difficult to prove in five or six hundred words:

The Great Train Robbery is the finest movie ever made.

or

James Cagney was more talented than any other actors, either before or after him.

or

Love Story was the worst film to come out of Hollywood's sordid history.

Narrow these topics down to less ambitious opinions such as:

The Great Train Robbery is an outstanding example of the silent film.

or

James Cagney was one of Hollywood's finest actors.

or

Although a box office smash, *Love Story* was no better than a grade B movie.

Remember, once you make the assertion, your job is to show why that opinion is so reasonable that thoughtful people must accept it. Don't create an impossible task.

Also, be sure your thesis is one you really believe in. Debaters may find value in arguing both sides of an issue, but you need only one viewpoint, and it might as well be one you feel comfortable with. You may be able to fake an argument for an idea you don't care about, but you'll never be as convincing as when you are truly enthusiastic about the topic.

Finally, make sure your thesis statement contains both a topic and some opinion about that topic. Since the purpose of your essay is to convince, your thesis must be carefully thought out. The following six guidelines will help you phrase your thesis sentence as clearly and compellingly as possible.

Checklist for Writers

1. *The thesis must be a full sentence.*

    Don't write "A national policy on drug abuse." This thesis names the topic but gives no clue as to what position the author is taking about a national policy on drug abuse.

    Instead, write "A national policy on drug abuse must meet five criteria." This thesis sentence is better because it not only names the topic but also expresses a specific opinion about that topic and hints that you might tell us what those criteria are.

2. *The thesis must be a declarative sentence rather than a question.*

    Don't write "Are racially mixed marriages a good idea?" Once you ask a question, you have invited the reader to answer with his or her own opinion. If the reader's ideas are different from yours, you are looking for trouble. Besides that, you still haven't told us what your ideas are on the subject.

Instead, write "Racially mixed marriages can succeed if the couple is prepared for the inevitable difficulties." Only a declaration like this, clearly giving your opinion, can function as a real thesis sentence. In addition, readers expect to learn about the inevitable difficulties.

3. *The thesis must state only one major idea.*

Don't write "Police promotion should be determined by examination only, and police in most cities are underpaid." This statement contains two separate opinions, and the only relationship is that both of them involve police officers. Save the second opinion for another essay, and concentrate on proving that your first idea is true.

Instead, write "Police promotion should be determined by examination only." This sounds like an opinion that you could support in the length of one essay. Your readers expect you to tell them why this is true.

4. *The thesis must state your idea with certainty.*

Don't write "I think the city police need more training." If you make that statement about city police, obviously you think it is true. Why tell us what is already obvious? "In my opinion," "It seems to me," and "I believe" are just as bad. Each carries with it the idea that this is "just" your opinion, as if there is something wrong with your ideas.

Instead, write "The city police need more training." This is a perfectly clear statement of your opinion and suggests that you may make specific recommendations.

5. *The thesis must be expressed in precise language.*

Don't write "The Lakewood College library is nice." The word nice has been so overused that it doesn't give a clue to what you really think of the library. Does it have a fine reference collection? Wonderful vending machines? Clean rest rooms?

Instead, write "The Lakewood College Library is a beautiful example of functional architecture." Now your readers know what you approve of and can look forward to an accurate description of the place.

6. *The thesis sentence must immediately suggest a clear and meaningful idea.*

Don't write "If human selfishness is put down, it can be helpful to anyone who is concerned." This sentence is so vague and the meaning so obscure that it could suggest any one of three or four ideas—or no idea at all.

Instead, write "Overcoming human selfishness could save many marriages." The language has been clarified, and the opinion is much more clear. Now, you can tell the reader what improvement will come about.

Because the thesis sentence expresses your attitude and because you want to persuade the reader to agree with you, your thesis sentence must first be perfectly clear in your own mind and then expressed in language that is both clear and concise.

SUMMARY

1. Picture every writing assignment as an opportunity to talk your reader into something.
2. Write out your point of view, your opinion, in the form of a thesis sentence.
3. Be sure you can support that opinion.
4. Word your opinion as clearly as possible.

DISCUSS

1. What are the major functions of a thesis sentence?
2. List the six characteristics of a good thesis sentence and explain why each is so important.

ACT

1. Name one topic on which you have a definite opinion.
   Example: "The condition of the streets in our town."
2. If necessary, narrow that topic to a subject you could explain in about five hundred words.
   Example: "The results of last winter's damage to our streets."
3. Keeping in mind the six guidelines from this chapter, write a thesis sentence you really believe in.
   Example: "The streets in our town are so full of potholes that they are a real danger to health and property."

Support Your Idea

If someone makes a statement with which you don't immediately agree, the normal reaction is to ask a few questions.

"What do you mean 'the United States should take the initiative in starting disarmament talks'? Why should we be first?"

"What makes you think 'students create most of their own problems with scheduling conflicts'? How do they do that? Why would they do that?"

If a speaker has some good reasons, you are usually willing to listen and perhaps be convinced that the idea has merit. On the other hand, if the answer is a weak "I don't know. I just think it's a good idea," or "I just think so, that's all," the speaker loses credibility and you lose respect for those views. One person's opinion is just as good as another's only if the person can support that opinion with some hard evidence.

Writing is no different. When you present one of your beliefs (the thesis statement), you must explain why you feel that way. Your writing needs specific support for any ideas you put forward, and that support comes in the form of topic sentences and the explanation of each topic sentence.

The body of a typical essay will present three or four good reasons why the thesis statement is true. That number gives the impression that you could come up with others if necessary. Once in a while, one very important, very convincing reason will be sufficient, but most essays will be more effective if you have several pieces of evidence to support your opinion.

Each of your three or four reasons will form the topic sentence of a separate paragraph, and each of those paragraphs will explain the reason thoroughly. Usually, the topic sentence will be the first sentence of the paragraph, and the remaining sentences can make up the explanation. A typical essay based on the thesis sentence and topic sentences might be arranged like this:

Arrangement:
  A. Thesis sentence.
  B. Reason 1 + four or five sentences of explanation.
  C. Reason 2 + four or five sentences of explanation.
  D. Reason 3 + four or five sentences of explanation.

Example:
A. (Thesis) Americans today do not take care of their health.
B. (Reason 1) They get no exercise. [This is followed by a paragraph about how Americans watch television, drive everywhere they go, and depend on labor-saving gadgets.]
C. (Reason 2) They eat the worst kinds of junk foods. [This is followed by a paragraph about the horrors of diets rich in Twinkies, nachos, and colas.]
D. (Reason 3) They smoke and drink too much. [This paragraph will tell about the degree to which people use tobacco and alcohol.]

By the time you develop those three paragraphs of support, it should be obvious to the dullest reader why you say Americans do not maintain their health.

Remembering Why You Feel That Way

If you have trouble coming up with topic sentences (reasons why your thesis is true), use the magic-word questions discussed in Section 2, Make Plans.

How? How do you know that? In what way is it true?
Why? Why is that true? Why do you say so?

Some topics work well with just "how," some with just "why," and some produce good ideas from either question.

Example:

Thesis: Capital punishment should be banned in all states.
     Why should capital punishment be banned?
     Reason 1. Mistakes cannot be corrected.
     Reason 2. The poor tend to be executed in greater numbers.
     Reason 3. The murder rate does not go down in states that have capital punishment.

Thesis: Written assignments tell teachers a lot about students.
     How do written assignments tell about students?
     Reason 1. Content can show a level of intelligence.

Reason 2. Mechanics (spelling and punctuation) show the kind of education you have.

Reason 3. The appearance of the paper shows something about the writer's values.

Thesis: College will be more difficult than high school.

Why will college be more difficult than high school?

Reason 1. College students are expected to be more mature.

Reason 2. College is supposed to train students to be more independent.

How will college be more difficult than high school?

Reason 3. Teachers give tests that cover more material.

Reason 4. Long-range assignments require more self-discipline.

Reason 5. Competition for grades is greater.

Try both *Why* and *How*, and use whatever combination seems most useful.

Explaining Your Reasons

Once you have your thesis statement and three or four reasons why you think it is true, the hard part is done. All you need to do now is develop four or five sentences to clarify or explain each topic (reason) sentence. If the idea is more complex, more sentences may be necessary. Adding a good example makes it even better.

If you have problems developing one of your topic sentences into a paragraph, try the same type of questioning you used to get the topic sentence. The only difference is that you have more freedom at this point. Instead of limiting yourself to how and why, expand your thinking to include any questions that seem appropriate.

In what way is this true?

When is this true?

Where is this true?

What makes this happen?

The following thesis and subpoints can be supported by applying and answering whichever questions seem appropriate.

Thesis: Supporting private schools through tuition tax credits would be harmful to everyone involved.

Reason 1. Tax credits would weaken our traditional free public schools.

Reason 2. We cannot afford the extra federal expense at this time.

Reason 3. The independence of private schools would be endangered.

Start with reason 1, "Tuition tax credits would weaken our traditional free public schools." By answering the question, "What makes this happen?" you can show why you believe it.

"Tuition tax credits would weaken our traditional free public schools. It is reasonable to expect that the prospect of having tuition paid by the government should attract many parents to private schools. For instance, my neighbor can't afford to send his children to our local parochial schools. However, if the government will reimburse him for half the expense, the offer will be pretty hard to resist. After all, he knows the schools are good, and he is already supporting them indirectly with his weekly church contributions. The problem here is that as more and more students desert their public schools, less and less financial support will be available. At first glance this may seem fair, but because of the variety of classes required by law, it costs nearly as much to educate fifteen as it does to educate thirty. The final result will be a situation in which the remaining public school children have to make do with half the minimal resources available. At a time when public schools are being attacked for doing a poor job, it makes no sense to abandon them as a lost cause."

In reason 3, the writer said that "The independence of private schools would be endangered." By answering the question, "In what way is this true?" she came up with a paragraph that explains why she believed what she said.

"The independence of private schools would be endangered. The federal government will have to set some sort of minimum educational standards before an institution can be called a qualified school. As soon as the prospective students have some of their tuition paid by the government, questionable schools will spring up all over, and all will claim to give the advantages of a private-school education with little of the extra expense. Many of them will be fly-by-night organizations, requiring more surveillance than any of our existing schools. The danger is that, as time goes on, the independence and diversity that our private schools so cherish will be lost to the bureaucratic control that always accompanies federal money."

SUMMARY

1. Find three or four reasons (topic sentences) why your thesis is true. Ask yourself *why* and *how* that thesis is true. Each of these reasons becomes the topic sentence for a support paragraph.
2. For each reason (topic sentence), develop four or five (or more) sentences that explain the topic sentence. Ask where, when, and in what way this is true. These, when added to the topic sentences, become the body of your essay. See page 18 for an outline showing how these elements fit together.

DISCUSS

1. Why is it important that people be able to support their opinions?
2. To what degree is one person's opinion just as good as another's?
3. What form should support for your thesis take?
4. What process can you use to produce topic sentences that support your thesis?
5. After writing topic sentences to support your thesis, how should you generate information that will become your supporting paragraphs?

ACT

1. Look back in this chapter at the sample thesis about tuition tax credits. Turn the thesis completely around so it asserts the opposite viewpoint and supports the concept of tuition tax credits. Write three topic sentences to support tuition tax credits.
2. Name one topic on which you have a definite opinion. If you like, use one of the following:
   a. smoking
   b. professional sports
   c. welfare
   d. disarmament
   e. television advertising
   State your opinion on this topic in the form of a thesis sentence. If necessary, consult the guidelines from Section 3, Use a Thesis Sentence.

3. Using this thesis sentence, write three topic sentences to support your idea. Show what questions (how, why) you asked about the thesis to determine the three topic sentences.
4. The goal of topic sentence development is to show why your thesis is true. For each topic sentence from step 3, show which questions you would answer to develop it.
   In what way is this true?
   When is this true?
   Where is this true?
   What makes this happen?

After each topic sentence, write all of the questions you'd ask and a full-sentence answer to each of them.

Be Specific

It's a pretty rare student who doesn't get papers back with suggestions from the teacher. You may be told to clean up the mechanical errors, use a simpler vocabulary, or eliminate some unnecessary words. But the most common complaint (and it's usually justified) is that the support given to topic sentences is too vague, too abstract, too general. In other words, your reasons aren't easy enough to understand.

Problems of vagueness or obscurity occur because you are dealing with ideas, and it's not easy to "see" an idea. You just can't easily picture abstractions such as "talented" or "ambitious" or "making demands." Even when you are able to create a mental picture of "talented" or "dedicated," you can never be sure it is the same picture someone else might conjure up. What you need is some method of grasping that picture, putting it into specific words, and getting it into the other person's mind with enough detail to be sure she or he sees the same picture.

E. B. White offered a solution. He said, "Don't write about man, write about *a* man." That's not always easy to do, and one way of going about it is to try the photographic approach. Students in writing courses always have the feeling that anything would be easier than another essay assignment. What would happen if, just once, you got an assignment like this one?

"Students, this week you will be doing a visual essay. After you have selected a subject, written your thesis sentence, and come up with three topic sentences that show why the thesis is true, you may check out one of these instant cameras that are on my desk. Find a scene or situation that shows exactly what you mean by your first topic sentence, and take a picture of it. Be sure that scene perfectly illustrates what you have in mind. Next, find some people or places that make perfect examples of your second and third topic sentences, and take pictures of them, too.

"For instance, if your first topic sentence is 'Dedication is absolutely necessary for the exceptional athlete,' you might look around until you find some person who exemplifies that dedication and take a picture of him or her. Take a picture of that athlete doing something that shows real dedication. Take a picture of her out running on the track on a hot July evening. Get close enough so that we can see the sweat pouring off her forehead.

"When you have one picture for each of your topic sentences, paste the photographs under their topic sentences on a sheet of paper. Hand them in on Friday."

Although the probability of your actually getting that assignment is fairly low, you can still use the concept in your writing. Put yourself in that situation. If you had to take a picture of someone or some situation that showed what you mean by your topic sentence, what would the picture look like? Draw a stick figure diagram if you like. Include all the details your imagination sees, but concentrate on the most important person or object in the picture.

Ask yourself the following questions about the information reaching your senses. Ignore any questions that don't seem appropriate.

Checklist for Writers

1. How are things positioned? How close are the people or objects? What is the relationship between parts of the scene?
2. How big is the main subject? What could you compare it or he or she to?
3. What colors are there? Which ones stand out the most? Tell the reader.
4. Is it moving? Which way? How fast? How smoothly?
5. What does it feel like? Soft? Smooth? Hot? Cold?
6. What sounds do you hear? Soft? Loud? Steady? Musical?
7. What does it smell or taste like? Sweet? Sour? Spicy? Compare it to something else.

Now write a description of that mental picture. Your paragraph should give the reader something tangible to think about as you explain why your subpoint is reasonable. Don't just tell him exceptional athletes must be dedicated to their training—show him.

You will probably still want to use a few sentences of straight explanation to support that topic sentence, but be sure to add something the mind can see. For instance, see what you could do with "Dedication is absolutely necessary, even for the exceptional athlete."

At five o'clock in the morning the quarter-mile track is deserted except for an old, yellowish collie searching under the bleachers. Neighborhood starlings have started chattering, signaling the official sunrise even though no light has broken through the purple clouds. From the scoreboard-end of the field, the sound of nylon on nylon comes whish, whish, whishing out of the semidarkness. The six-foot, blue-hooded figure picks up speed as she approaches and the nylon sound flows together as Marcy turns her seventeenth lap into a sprint. The dusty-dry smell of disturbed gravel hangs in the air long after she is gone.

You can use this same approach to make almost any idea seem more real. If you need to show that college students learn independence by making decisions for themselves, draw a picture of someone who might like some parental support but needs to make a personal decision without any outside advice. Describe the scene and feel free to throw in some dialogue.

If you want to tell about the student who learned to make decisions by shopping for her own food, draw at least a mental picture of how she spent all her money on exotic foods, learning too late that this left no cereal for breakfast or bread for lunch. "Write a picture" of Jeannie searching the refrigerator for some lunch and finding only pickled snails and avocado dip. It will be much more effective than the bland "They learn to make decisions through being allowed to make mistakes."

SUMMARY

When you write about ideas, such as patriotism or loyalty, specific examples are essential to making certain that your reader understands you. One way to communicate your understanding of an abstract idea is to create a mental photograph and describe that picture for your reader.

DISCUSS

1. What is the most common complaint teachers have about student writing?
2. What is the meaning of "Don't write about man, write about *a man*"?
3. How can you give the reader something tangible to think about when you discuss abstract terms such as *talented* or *ambitious?*
4. What kinds of details should be included in a description so that the reader will have something tangible to think about?

ACT

At the end of Section 4, you wrote a thesis and topic sentence outline. After each topic sentence you wrote the answer to questions such as "When is this true?" and "What makes this happen?" Choose one of these topic sentences, (or write a new one) and develop it into a photographic paragraph. Consult the Checklist for Writers on page 21 and jot down the details you want your reader to picture mentally—size, color, movement, texture, sound, smell, taste and so on. What could you compare it to? Now write a description of that mental picture. Make the topic sentence the first sentence of your paragraph, and then show why or when or how it is true.

2

The Alpha and the Omega

You may have heard someone say of a classmate, "Terri thinks she is the alpha and the omega of the volleyball team." In a more admiring tone, a film critic might say, "Michael Douglas is the alpha and the omega of this new movie."

The first is a negative comment, suggesting that Terri's concern about the team begins and ends with herself. The second is a compliment, suggesting that Michael Douglas overshadows everyone else in the film.

Alpha and *omega* are the first and last letters of the Greek alphabet, and they have long been a familiar way of referring to the beginning and ending of almost anything. Of course, the phrase implies that the first and last parts, the introduction and the conclusion, are more important than anything that comes between.

The introduction and conclusion of your essay may not overshadow what comes between, but they are important—important enough to deserve special attention.

Introductions

Although it may sound natural to write an introduction before you write anything else, it's not always a good idea. If you write the introduction first, you may have an incomplete idea of exactly what you're leading into. Wouldn't it be easier to wait until the essay is more complete and then think of a great way to get into the topic? After all, one of the main purposes of an introduction is to interest the reader in the topic.

The introduction has three purposes. It should:

1. Get the reader's attention
2. Introduce the topic in a natural sounding manner
3. Make a smooth transition into the body of the paper

Introductions can have an unlimited variety of forms, but for now, consider the most useful one—the all-purpose generic introduction.

Generic Introductions

When you're having a relaxed conversation with friends and you want to bring up a subject without being too obvious, you mention a topic that is generally related. For example, if you want to talk about a jazz festival that is coming up, you might start by mentioning something about music. If you want to talk about a friend's marriage, you might first bring up the topic of dating. Or if you want to talk about a particular class you'll be taking next semester, you may broach the topic of requirements for various colleges.

These related topics almost always allow you to steer the conversation in the direction you want. It's a short step from the discussion of college requirements, for example, to the subject of fourth-year math. In a one-sided conversation like an essay, steering is a piece of cake. What is more, there is nothing underhanded about this. It's an accepted method of moving from one topic to another.

Remember, in your essay you have the advantage of writing the introduction last. You already have a thesis sentence, and the body of the paper has been completed. Approach this introduction in three steps.

Checklist for Writers

1. Pick one idea or term out of your existing thesis sentence.
2. Make an innocent-sounding, innocuous, non-controversial comment about that idea.
3. Develop that innocent-sounding sentence with some additional comments that either explain what you mean or illustrate the truth of the statement, all the while working the discussion toward the thesis sentence itself.

For instance, suppose you want to work your way into the following statement:

The ability to locate and use outside resources is a daily requirement in Ms. Knight's classroom.

That thesis sentence contains at least five elements: (1) ability, (2) locate, (3) resources, (4) classroom, and (5) requirement. Any one of those elements can be used to lead the conversation (essay) into that thesis statement. If you can use two or three elements at once, your job becomes even easier. For example:

Several *abilities* are *required* for success in college preparatory *classes*. Most classes call for good note-taking and test-taking skills, but many have additional requirements because of their unique purposes. For instance, science calls for one type of talent and a foreign language requires another. To further complicate matters, some teachers have their own pet interests and requirements. The ability to locate and use outside resources in Ms. Knight's classroom is a daily requirement.

The generic introduction will work with any topic, no matter how difficult the subject matter. Just pick out one aspect of the thesis, make an inoffensive comment about it, and let that lead you naturally into the thesis statement, just as if you were trying to change the subject of a conversation.

Specialized Introductions

In addition to the generic introduction, there are several specialized introductions. Quotations, personal experiences, famous-person anecdotes, questions, and refutations can all be used to lead into a thesis sentence. The following examples all bring up the topic of people's lack of taste: "We are wallowing in a barnyard of bad taste and don't seem to mind all that much."

Quotations

Use a quote from a well-known person to bring up the topic.

Arnold Bennett once said, "Bad taste is better than no taste at all," but I'm not sure he would want to make the distinction today. It's serious enough when we are incapable of discerning and appreciating beauty, but we seem to have reached a point where we are incapable of reacting to sheer ugliness. We are wallowing in a barnyard of bad taste and don't seem to mind all that much.

Personal Experiences

Relate an incident in which you were involved that reminds you of the topic.

Standing alone in the shopping center, I was engaged in the diversion most malls serve so well: people watching. The man in the red-and-black T-shirt strode along the walkway and was almost past me before I noticed the message on his chest. It was a huge map of Japan with two stars marking cities and, above it, the line "Two Bombs Were Not Enough." Whatever the motivation for his tastelessness, he was a perfect representative of all those ugly little bumper-sticker and T-shirt messages that assault us each day. Every one of them makes us a little less sensitive to the next assault. We are wallowing in a barnyard of bad taste and don't seem to mind all that much.

Famous Person Anecdotes

Tell a story involving a well-known person.

Dan Aykroyd, a long-time regular on "Saturday Night Live," does a one-man skit in which he satirizes television commercials by trying to sell his audience the Super Bassomatic Blender. According to Aykroyd, this labor-saving device cuts down on preparation time when serving fish to your family. Instead of scaling and gutting the fish, Aykroyd merely drops one whole, live bass into the Super Bassomatic Blender and flips the switch. Instantly, the fish is pureed and ready for the table. Aykroyd then offers up the brown liquid mess as a new culinary treat. Any supposed humor in this skit comes from the audience's discomfort as they think about what has happened to the fish and what they are being asked to drink. We are wallowing in a barnyard of bad taste and don't seem to mind all that much.

Questions

Ask a question about the topic.

> Must we stand around quietly while classmates come to school wearing shirts decorated with tasteless and suggestive messages? I don't object to this crudity because of any assumed superiority or amazing ACT scores. It doesn't take a snob to recognize that some things should be beneath human dignity. In fact, some irritations are so maddening that even the most timid among us has an obligation to stand up and say out loud, "This is shoddy, and I am offended." We are wallowing in a barnyard of bad taste and don't seem to mind all that much.

Refutations

Present the opposition's main argument against your thesis and show why this is wrong.

> Some people claim that a certain amount of tackiness is good for children. After all, they are going to have to live in the real world whether we approve or not. The theory is that, if they are exposed to something, they will learn how to deal with it. The evidence I see all around shouts down that theory. We don't learn how to combat tackiness or deal with it. We just get used to it, and that's not the same thing. We are wallowing in a barnyard of bad taste and don't seem to mind all that much.

Your choice of introduction is entirely personal so long as it accomplishes the three major purposes of an introduction.

1. Get the reader's attention.
2. Introduce the topic in a natural-sounding manner.
3. Make a smooth transition into the body of the paper.

The length of the introduction depends more than anything else on the length of the body of the essay. If the whole essay is only five or six paragraphs long, the introduction should be no more than one paragraph. If the essay is five pages long, the introduction should be about one page long. Usually, the introduction should be no more than 15 to 20 percent of the total essay, but it could be more or less if you feel it is necessary.

Whatever your decisions about the content, the kind, and the length of your introduction, the whole job will go more smoothly if you wait until the rest of the essay is done.

SUMMARY

Writing the introduction may be easier if you wait until the body of your essay is complete. The conversational generic introduction is a safe choice for introducing almost any topic. In addition, quotations, personal experiences, famous-person anecdotes, questions, and refutations of the opposition's main argument are all specialized introductions that can provide variety.

DISCUSS

1. Why might it be a good idea to write the introduction after completing the body of the essay?
2. What is the generic introduction? Explain how it is used.
3. Name and describe five specialized introductions.
4. How can you determine the proper length for an introduction?

ACT

Read the following thesis sentences.
1. Many people get divorced without sufficient reason.
2. The space program is not making sufficient progress.
3. The prison system needs a complete overhaul.
4. Drug addiction is responsible for much of today's crime.

Think of several methods you could use to introduce each thesis. Choose three of the methods discussed in this chapter and, using each method, write an introduction of at least five sentences. The last sentence of the introduction must be your thesis statement. You may use one or more of these thesis sentences, or some of your own.

Conclusions

Much advice to student writers fails to make one fact sufficiently clear—every essay needs a real, live conclusion. At the very least, one sentence is necessary to bind the ideas of your essay together. Just as you needed an introduction to bring up your main point, you need a conclusion to nail it down.

The next problem is how to go about writing the conclusion. Let's start with a few general guidelines and then move on to some specific suggestions.

First, the shorter the conclusion the better—within reason. This will be your readers' last impression of the essay. Do them a favor and keep it relevant, clear, and concise.

Second, the conclusion should usually be in the form of a multisentence paragraph, and that means it will need a topic sentence just like any other paragraph.

Third, the topic sentence should be an imaginative reminder or rewording of the thesis statement. It should bring together all the aspects of the essay and leave the reader with a clear understanding of your viewpoint. This is your last chance to reach the reader, and even if your specific reasons have been forgotten, the thesis should remain firmly in mind.

Last, your conclusion can do more than just tie together main ideas. It should make one final, significant point. What point that might be is entirely your choice, but it should flow smoothly and logically from the information in your essay.

Five Methods

There are five specific methods for ending your essay: offering recommendations, making predictions, calling for action, quoting a stimulating source, and summarizing your main points.

Recommendations

If your essay is critical of a situation or event, you may want to suggest needed changes. For example, if your essay is about the weaknesses of your school's library, you might end with recommendations for improving the situation.

> Our library has several glaring weaknesses that must be corrected. Educational requirements for new staff should be more demanding, more space should be provided for students' studying and research, and the entire reference section should be updated. Only if these changes are made can we hope to attract top quality students and faculty.

Predictions

If you wrote an essay on the prevalence of student cheating, you might end with a prediction about what effect this will have on future job performance.

> Cheating is out of control at this school. It's hard to ignore the long-term effects on engineers who have never learned to write clear, concise reports. And imagine the kind of impression people get from teachers who can't speak clearly or correctly. Office managers whose daily memos are full of usage errors lose the respect of their subordinates. Cheaters hurt themselves most, and the punishment will be more than sufficient.

Calls to Action

If you wrote an essay about environmental problems, you might finish with an invitation for people to get busy and improve the situation.

> The Cedar River has become a source of danger to all of us, but we can do something about it. Call local companies and question them about the source of the problem. Write to executives of those manufacturing plants and let them know about the threat of legal action against their activities. And last, keep in touch with your state legislators. Keep them informed, because they are our best hope for doing something about the problem.

Stimulating Quotes

If you have written an essay about the rise of Fascism, you may want to close with a memorable, thought-provoking quote.

> Sydney Harris, the newspaper columnist, wrote, "There are moral imbeciles just as there are mental imbeciles; but while the latter are recognized as having a congenital defect and are put away for their own good, the former often acquire great power and acclaim in the world—yet the man born with a deficient moral nerve is a thousand times more dangerous than the mental defective."

Summaries

If your essay is very long and complex, readers may appreciate a summary of the main points. The summary conclusion is probably the least interesting, however, and should be used sparingly.

> College represents a big change for thousands of students every year. As I have indicated, those students (1) are expected to be fairly mature, (2) must develop independence, (3) need self-discipline, (4) have to take more difficult tests, and (5) must compete for grades. Almost everyone finds college more difficult than high school.

Conclusions can be just as challenging to write as introductions. Whatever form you choose, be sure to close with a thought that reinforces the main idea of your essay.

SUMMARY

End essay with a short paragraph of conclusion. It should leave the reader with a sense of finality as well as a clear understanding of your viewpoint. Recommendations, predictions, calls to action, stimulating quotes, or summaries all can reinforce the main idea of your essay.

DISCUSS

1. List and explain the four guidelines governing the use of conclusions.
2. Name the five types of conclusions, and suggest a type of essay for which each might be appropriate.

ACT

Look back at the three introductions you wrote at the end of the last section. Write a conclusion for each.

The Whole Essay

Now that you have learned about the three parts of an essay—the introduction, the body, and the conclusion—step back and take a look at the assignment as a whole.

Remember, you can write the parts of your essay in any order you're comfortable with. The steps suggested here do not reflect the order of the parts in your final copy, but if you follow these steps, your work will be much easier.

Checklist for Writers

1.   Choose a topic. If a topic has been assigned, count it a blessing and be grateful.
2.   State your thesis in a sentence. Writing a complete sentence forces you to say something specific about your topic.
3.   Write three or four sentences explaining why you believe your thesis is true. Each of these sentences will become a topic sentence in the body of your paper.
4.   Develop a paragraph of support for each of your topic sentences. Be as specific as you can.
5.   Arrange your supporting paragraphs in the most logical or powerful order. Experiment with different combinations.
6.   Write an introduction. You'll find it much easier to tell your readers where you are going now that you've been there.
7.   Write a conclusion. Keep it short and snappy.

Write the parts of your essay in any order you wish. It's great when the right words come to you in a flash of inspiration. Get them down on paper quickly—inspiration is too rare to pass up.

SUMMARY

Think of your essay as a structure you put together in a specific pattern, somewhat like designing a house. No architect feels overly confined when we expect a front door and a back door, and we think it's perfectly normal to insist on a bathroom and kitchen. Expressing yourself should be easier because the structure frees you from concern about how to arrange ideas, and it imposes a discipline on your thoughts, both of which can only lead to clearer thinking.

DISCUSS
❝❝

Read the following essay and be prepared to discuss the questions that follow it.

Dianne Smart
Senior Composition
September 10, 19____

Pot or Not?

Every time the legal system develops a problem handling people's behavior, someone suggests that maybe we should just legalize the behavior. Naturally, with steadily rising drug abuse and the major crimes that accompany such abuse, there is talk of legalizing marijuana. If this were to occur, many unforeseen problems would arise, similar to those that accompany the legal sale of alcohol. Legalizing marijuana would be a tragic mistake for our society.

If marijuana became legal, drug use would begin at an earlier age. As of now, drug dealers are somewhat limited in the areas in which they can sell drugs because they want to remain hidden from the law. However, if legalization did occur, drugs could be sold everywhere, including elementary and junior high schools. We have enough of a problem now, without having high school students selling to their younger friends. Children who have no way of getting marijuana would then have no problem finding it, and drug use would begin at an even earlier age. The same sort of situation can be seen in those states where alcoholic beverages are legal for 18-year-olds. The 18-year-olds sell to their younger friends, and eventually the availability trickles down to the elementary school. Alcohol is much more available to children than most adults realize, and abuse is known to exist among elementary students. The same thing would happen if marijuana were legalized.

In addition to children using drugs, law-abiding adults might begin sampling legalized marijuana. Many people avoid drugs now simply because they are illegal. Others fear that drugs might harm their bodies. However, if Congress legalized marijuana, many citizens would feel unrestrained in using drugs, and others would feel it was possible to smoke marijuana without harming themselves. Again the 18-year-olds illustrate the problem. Many who would not normally drink will begin to do so simply because it has been made available.

Such legal accessibility leads to a third problem. The addiction rate among drug users would increase. Again, because of the increased availability of marijuana, usage would be much more continuous since drugs could be more easily purchased. Drug dealers, competing for sales, would drive prices down. Marijuana would become much more affordable, so people would buy more of it. It would be used more often, causing the addiction rate to rise dramatically. Though there is doubt about marijuana being physically addictive, there is no doubt that it is psychologically addictive.

Last, the lives of innocent people would be greatly endangered if marijuana became legal. The drug would be more frequently used in public, and a problem similar to "Operating a Motor Vehicle While Intoxicated" would arise. Just as alcohol abusers too often appear behind the wheels of cars, planes, and boats, marijuana users would very likely do the same. Passengers and other innocent drivers would be killed, and the number of drug-related deaths would certainly increase.

If marijuana becomes a legal drug like alcohol, younger people will begin using it, addiction will increase, and innocent people could be harmed by drug abusers. These problems pose strong arguments against legalizing marijuana.

1. Identify the thesis statement of the essay. What question is the thesis sentence answering?

2. List the supporting points of the essay. What question does each supporting point answer about the thesis statement?

3. Choose two of the supporting points and write a brief criticism, telling how well you think each is developed. Explain whether each paragraph answers the questions raised by the topic sentence.

4. Which type of introduction does this essay use? What other type of introduction might work here?

5.   What type of conclusion does the essay use? What other type of conclusion might work well?

Write an essay of 500 to 700 words following the steps described in this chapter. Write down your responses to each step and hand these in with your completed essay. Your teacher may prefer to check each step before you move on to the next one.

You may choose one of the following topics or select a topic of your own. Whatever topic you select, however, be sure to narrow it to fit the required length.

A well-known sports figure
Interracial marriage
Academic credit for music participation
Federal tax reform
High school athletics
Dating rituals

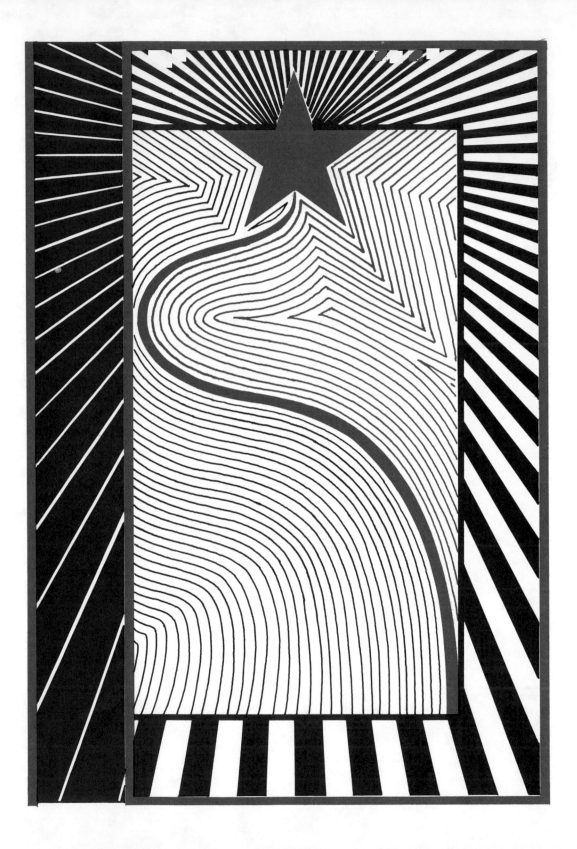

3

Improvement Is the New Goal

Now that you have your assignment down on paper, there is a decision to be made. You can either settle for this essay as it is, or you can go all the way and try to make it something really special.

If this is a short assignment that's due very soon, you may not have a choice. A paper due this afternoon won't get much serious revision. In that case, at least take time to read it over and eliminate obvious problems. In the first attempt at putting an idea into words, almost anyone's thought is a little unclear, and you will surely need to straighten out a snarled sentence or two. Check the spelling, check the punctuation, and be realistic about the time available.

Often, however, you will have more than twenty-four hours between receiving the assignment and handing it in. For most major college papers and for the assignments in this book, you will have anywhere from several days to a week or more. That is plenty of time to do some serious rereading and rewriting.

Some Don'ts and Some Do's

On a second reading you may discover that your paper is short on specific details and examples. If this is the case, take the time to add them. Use an incident that shows what you mean. Explain more fully if that will help. Your greatest improvement, though, is going to come from actually making this beautiful piece of writing *shorter.* There are three types of words you should try to eliminate when possible.

Foreign words are necessary occasionally when there is no precise English equivalent. But a problem arises when writers try to decorate their work with elegant or pretentious vocabulary and include foreign words and phrases that add nothing. Most of the time this is a simple case of showing off, but whatever the motivation, it is hard on the reader. Cross out meaningless little beauties like *mariage de convenance, laissez faire,* and *enfant terrible*. Almost everyone can figure them out, true, but most readers already know about marriages of convenience, noninterference, and young terrors.

Worse things than *slang* can creep into your paper, but try to remember your audience. Will they appreciate your pioneering efforts in the language? If not, you may be better off to err on the side of conservatism.

Be honest with yourself. Is this slang accomplishing something special, like creating a comfortable mood, or is it just laziness? Using precise English is difficult, and a great deal of slang simply substitutes words that come easiest to mind for the right words.

If you must use slang, do it without any attempt at justification. Don't make more of your little sin by putting it in quotation marks or underlining it. That looks as if you are either trying to be cute or feeling guilty about using an inferior word. Neither is something you want to be accused of.

> Search and destroy. Believe it or not, you ought to have a sneaking suspicion that, in the final analysis, some drastic action might turn up a clinker or two. It stands to reason that you will find original wordings few and far between. That's the bottom line. Give it the acid test. It'll boggle your mind.

Read that paragraph again. You'll probably realize it doesn't say much. As with most *cliches,* that string of words is designed more than anything else to cover a lack of original effort. Avoid cliches like the plague.

Now here's some positive advice.

Read your paper out loud. Often an awkward-sounding word or phrase will be hidden until you hear it. You may be too familiar with your creation to recognize some real problems. Reading aloud helps.

If a sentence sounds hopelessly awkward, don't try to cross out a word here or there. It won't be enough. The problem is usually deeper than a few odd words. Start over. Throw the words up in your mind and let them come down in a fresh order. Play with the possibilities. Aim to say the idea in a completely new way.

Have a friend read your essay. Here is where you find out who your real friends are. In junior high you may have compared papers with your friends "to see how they did it." Half the time the purpose was to bolster your sagging confidence, but this basically sound process also works to find out if your meaning is clear to someone else. Explain the purpose of the assignment and see if a reader can understand what you are talking about. Is your argument clear?

Check the spelling. Save this for last because the earlier reading may turn up several spelling errors. Now that the paper is in pretty good shape, read it backwards. That's right. Backwards. Start at the end, and read in reverse. That way you view one word at a time and won't get distracted by the flow of a sentence. Give each word just a glance and go on. Mark questionable words and get out your spelling dictionary. Of course, spelling has nothing to do with content, but people will judge you by it.

Writing is hard work, and good writing calls for some tedious rereading and checking over what you have accomplished. Though there is little chance you will get rid of every cliche, careless piece of slang, awkward phrase, or misspelling, rereading is one of those jobs in which the results are directly proportional to the effort. Plan on reading all your papers several times before handing them in.

SUMMARY

Several types of words should be eliminated from your writing. Get rid of unnecessary foreign words, purposeless slang, and all cliches. Read your paper aloud and listen for awkward-sounding words and phrases. Have a friend read it to see if your meaning is unclear at any point. Finally, check the spelling.

DISCUSS

1. Name and explain three types of words that should be avoided in your writing. Give an original example of each.
2. What are three specific steps you can take to improve your essay?

ACT

1. Read the following paragraphs. What would you do to clarify the main ideas and communicate more fully? Keep in mind your answers to the discussion questions above.

> In order to understand the word *easy,* a definition must be applied that will explain the word more comprehensibly. Easy: the sum total of one's skill and knowledge of a subject channeled into a single objective.
>
> A horse stretching and biting his side may look for all intents and purposes as if the horse is just getting comfortable or has an itch. Faux pas. To me a mental alarm is set off. These are the first signs of sickness.

2. Read the following essay. What would you do to clarify the main ideas and communicate more clearly?

Curfews

Teenagers are given too many rules. If they are expected to be responsible and become even more responsible, they should be allowed to handle their own time. Curfews restrict teens' responsibility and freedom needlessly.

Teens can learn responsibility from managing their own time. They should learn to manage their time so that they could get enough sleep, do homework, and relax. If, for example, they stayed up too late, they would become tired and go to bed earlier.

Insomniacs could be doing many things instead of lieing in bed. I think everyone is an occasional insomniac. Then their curfew prevents them from doing anything because they have to be in bed. If your awake, you might as well be getting something accomplished.

Teens can and will do what they want in spite of what time they have to be home. Many parents set curfews to try to prevent their teenagers from getting into trouble. Kids can do the same things in the day that they can late at night. If they were going to drink, for instance, it's just as easy to drink at one in the afternoon as it is at one in the morning. Curfews won't change what kids do, just the time they do it.

Teenagers shouldn't have curfews. They should be allowed to be responsible for themselves.

Eliminate Unnecessary Information

Donald Hall, poet and author of over fifty books, once said, "Less is more, in prose as in architecture." That statement sounds unlikely when you've just been told to write an essay of 500 or 1,000 words. But consider the implications. Often, you approach an assignment like that with confusion about your real purpose. Is the purpose to explain something to readers, or is it to string 1,000 words one after the other to reach a minimum requirement? You can easily run up the word count by throwing in all kinds of unnecessary information. If that information distracts the reader from your thesis statement, you need to start cutting. No doubt, less may be more.

Sometimes, the addition of unnecessary information in an essay is the result of writing by free association. Putting ideas on paper just as they come to mind can be a big help, especially if you have trouble getting started, but it also tends to draw in much excess information. Your essay is not a laundry bag. You have to be selective and throw out even the most hilarious anecdotes or poignant personal experiences if they don't add to the purpose of your essay. That a piece of information is true doesn't mean it belongs.

For example, if you wrote an essay titled "Cheating Is Out of Control in This School," you would want to give several examples of cheating you had witnessed. That seems relevant. It might also be relevant to add the idea that some people seem unable to stop cheating, but there is a line you must not cross.

It is not relevant, for instance, to tell about a distant relative who cheated his way through high school and college, began work as an investment counselor, developed a gambling habit, bilked customers out of thousands of dollars, went to jail, lost his wife and children, and eventually committed suicide. This may be interesting, but it has nothing to do with the evidence that proves "Cheating Is Out of Control in This School." If you include a story like this, you are telling readers more than they need or want to know.

There is usually little danger that a writer who has gone through the steps of stating a thesis and developing three or four supporting topic sentences will get altogether off the subject, but it is common for writers to include many chatty little tidbits that add nothing to the evidence and may instead distract the reader from the strength of that evidence. Examples are absolutely necessary, but they must illustrate the truth of your topic sentence, not some loosely related idea.

This student, writing on the subject of what makes a good teacher, used Mr. Kenney as an example.

> Mr. Kenney is probably the single most inspiring teacher I have. He teaches science courses, but the specific courses and the facts we learn are nowhere near as important as the excitement created by his own love of the subject. He lures us into loving science almost as much as we love him. I only wish I had been so lucky in social studies. Most of the social studies teachers are nice, and they seem well prepared, but none of them make the class come alive, except maybe Ms. Nijim. Mr. Kenney has me so interested that I spend hours studying related material in the library when I really should be finishing my algebra assignments. Since Mr. Kenney is over 60, I assume that he will be retiring in the next few years. Hopefully, there will be others to carry on the tradition of teachers who make their students love learning.

The writer adds material only minimally related to the essay's point. For instance, he tells us about his bad fortune in selecting social studies teachers. We don't need to know about the strong and weak points of other teachers—only of Mr. Kenney. The fact that the excitement generated by Mr. Kenney causes the author to skip algebra assignments is, at best, of questionable relevance. In addition, Mr. Kenney's retirement and the question of whether he can be replaced don't add to our knowledge of what makes an inspirational teacher. The question is still "What's so inspirational about Mr. Kenney?"

The following paragraph leaves out the irrelevant material and adds some examples of Mr. Kenney's teaching style.

> Mr. Kenney is probably the most inspirational teacher I have. He teaches science courses, but the specific courses and facts we learn are nowhere near as important as the excitement created by his own love of the subject. One day he took the whole class on a field trip to collect edible plants. We ended up at his home, where we prepared and ate a meal made entirely of plants we had gathered along the way. In another class the students tested themselves by conduct-

ing contests. At the end of one unit, they designed paper airplanes and flew them out a second-story window. The winner's plane flew almost a whole block before touching ground. Mr. Kenney lures us into loving science almost as much as we love him.

That paragraph does stay on the topic of Mr. Kenney's inspirational teaching, but what would you do if those examples of original teaching practices were not available? The answer should be obvious by now. As Donald Hall said, "Less is more." Cut the paragraph short and use only what is directly related to your point.

SUMMARY

As a second step in improving your writing, cut out any unnecessary information. Each example must directly illustrate the point you are making. In fact, every paragraph and every sentence must in some way support your thesis statement.

DISCUSS

1. Explain the significance of "Less is more, in prose as in architecture."
2. Why do writers often include unnecessary information? Explain.

ACT

Rewrite the following paragraphs to provide better support. You will need to cut irrelevant information and supply new material. Your purpose is to show why the topic sentence is true.

Our streets are in terrible shape. Ever since the spring thaw, chuckholes have been ruining tires and front suspensions all over our town. The storm sewers are inadequate to carry off standing water, and pedestrians are constantly splashed by passing cars. Every time you try to complain to City Hall, the phones are busy. If you can get through to someone, they don't know what can be done about it.

The crime rate in this town is out of control. It is no longer safe to walk down even Main Street at night. Muggings are a constant threat. A great part of the blame has to go to the municipal utility company, which is responsible for our inadequate street lighting. They are also very slow about repairing malfunctioning traffic signals, and this causes accidents. With the low conviction rate for accused criminals, it's no wonder the police have such poor morale.

FOR YOUR JOURNAL

Donald Hall's comment, "Less is more, in prose as in architecture" was not 100 percent original. In fact, many people have expressed a similar opinion. In 1855 Robert Browning wrote "Less is more" about the work of Andrea Del Sarto, a Renaissance Florentine painter. And almost twenty-five hundred years earlier, Hesiod, a Greek poet, said, "Fools, they do not even know how much more is the half than the whole."

Can things be overdone? What happens when they are overdone? In a page or two of your journal, name and explain as many activities as you can in which "less is more." Be sure to include specific examples you have observed.

Eliminate Unnecessary Words

Sydney Smith, a British writer, said, "In composing, as a general rule, run your pen through every other word you have written; you have no idea what vigor it will give your style." Smith was exaggerating, but if writing is a hellish occupation, wordiness is the devil behind it. Writers can get so flustered by a blank sheet of paper that they are thrilled with any words that fill the void.

Wordiness is sometimes the result of being told to write the way you talk. Bad advice. People sometimes fill silences with empty phrases, and that's understandable when they must think on their feet. But writing gives you time to create a message that's better than speech. It should at least give the impression of ease and hide the fact that you weren't really too sure of yourself the first time through.

Look at a piece of your writing and see if there are any words or phrases you could remove without harming the meaning. Is there a shorter way to say it? For instance, the cliche "at this point in time" easily becomes "now." If a word or phrase doesn't really help, it should be dropped.

The following list of wordy phrases and their shorter equivalents is far from complete. Study it, though, until you have a feel for how much more direct and honest the shorter version is. If you can recognize the unnecessary or redundant element in each of these examples, you should be able to spot any problems in your own writing.

Wordy	Direct
a.c. or d.c. current	a.c. or d.c.
advance forward	advance
advance planning	planning
at an early date	soon
at this point in time	now
accompanied by	with
appreciate your informing me	please tell me
at all times	always
at your earliest possible convenience	soon
a large number of	many
as a result of	because
audible to the ear	audible
basically and fundamentally	(pick either one)
brief in duration	brief
before too long	soon
begin again	resume
be in a position to	can
bring to a conclusion	finish
carry out experiments	experiment
complete monopoly	monopoly
collect together	collect
cooperate together	cooperate
desirable benefits	(what other kind are there?)
due to the fact that	because
during the time that	while
debate about	debate
descend down	descend
end result	result
empty out	empty
enter into	enter
few in number	few
following after	following
first initiated	started
face up to	face
head up	head
in the near future	soon
in a range of from 20 to 30	20 to 30
in this day and age	now
in the event of	if
it could be said that	(delete)
I would like you to know that	(delete)

it is interesting to note that	(delete)
in connection with	with
many different ways	many ways
make an exception for	except
minimize as far as possible	minimize
most of the time	usually
month of August	August
modern youth of today	modern youth
miss out on	miss
meet up with	meet
open up	open
of an indefinite nature	indefinite
perceive with the eye	see
produce an increase in	raise
provide proof for	prove
pair of twins	twins
perform an examination	examine
raced quickly	race (slowly?)
red in color	red
return back	return
short in height	short
small in size	small
surrounded on all sides	surrounded
succeed in doing	do
soon in time	soon
three weeks in duration	three weeks
to be in agreement	agree
take note of	note
to make an improvement	improve
to be of the opinion that	think; believe
visible to the eye	visible

As a writer, taking a scalpel to your creative offspring is your most difficult job. You know how hard it was to fill that page in the first place. You remember the rush you felt as the words finally came and flowed onto the paper. They all looked beautiful. You loved them.

But they're not really children. They're excess mortar between the bricks. They're ugly paint running down the canvas, ruining your whole picture. If you clean it up now, no one will know what you've been up to, and when it's all over, you'll look a whole lot more intelligent.

SUMMARY

When people speak, they tend to fill silences with meaningless words and phrases. Writing and revising, on the other hand, give you the chance to pare the wordiness that comes so naturally and is so easily overlooked in first and even second drafts.

DISCUSS

1. Name two causes of wordiness in student writing.
2. Writers of business letters often ask you to answer "at your earliest convenience" when "soon" is just as good. Politicians say, "I have arrived at the opinion that" instead of "I think." And half the speeches given in the United States include "at this point in time" when "now" is perfectly clear. Why have so many wordy phrases developed into cliches?

ACT

Rewrite the following sentences. Cut out all the wasted words and phrases so that you say the same thing more directly and economically.

1. Twenty-five years ago in the past computers were unheard of and most people knew nothing about them.
2. School district consolidation would mean that athletic teams would also combine together.
3. The first baseman hit a home run that didn't start to descend down until it was way over the fence.
4. I think you should refer back to the original directions.
5. The tank struggled to advance forward through the soft, damp, wet sand.
6. Always return your library books back to the library.
7. Jim's winter coat is too large in size for his frame.
8. Shelly repeated again what she said before.
9. His convertible is a green car.
10. This anonymous poem was written by an unknown author.
11. I just passed the test recently.
12. Her fiance, the man she'll marry, is a little shorter in height than she is.
13. The candidates have revised and changed their final positions over and over.
14. This plan of action is unique and different.
15. Jim attempted to start the car which was not running.

Keep It Simple

During World War II the United States Civil Defense Agency spent a lot of time preparing civilians for the possibility of sabotage, bombing, even invasion. Blackouts were common as a defense against nighttime bombing raids, and signs were posted all over public buildings. True to their calling as bureaucrats, government writers created such messages as "Illumination must be extinguished when premises are vacated."

President Roosevelt, not one to ignore idiocy, shot back, "Damn it, why can't they say 'Put out the lights when you leave'?"

Like most people, Roosevelt was angered by what he saw as a deliberate attempt to impress readers with flowery or elegant language. "Put out the lights" was just as good and far less distracting.

Elegant writing is usually intended to impress readers rather than communicate with them. The writer needs to feel important, and the readers suffer mightily for it. Poorly educated people often use inflated language in an attempt to appear more learned, but some of the worst offenders are highly educated people who should know better.

Nothing draws criticism faster than a pompous attitude, and writers should be alert to the possibility. Whether the sinner is a teacher, lawyer, doctor, or student, the reaction is the same and the disdain is usually well deserved. Now is the time to make certain inflated language doesn't become a problem for you.

Occasionally, big words do have a more precise meaning or are more poetic. But for most essay writing, simple, direct language will better serve your purpose.

Flowery Language	Simple Language
abate	decrease
answer is in the affirmative	yes
advent	coming
assistance	help
behest	request
beg to differ	disagree
cognizant of	aware
commence	begin
compensation	pay

considerable magnitude	big
dwell	live
duly noted	noted
delineate	describe
exhibit a tendency toward	tend to
endeavor	try
facilitate	help
floral offering	flowers
germane	relevant
hiatus	gap
in close proximity	near
in lieu of	instead of
inquire	ask
intermingle	mix
in view of the foregoing circumstances	therefore
it is incumbent on	must
kindly	please
make the acquaintance of	meet
multitudinous	many
notwithstanding the fact that	although
nuptials	wedding
obviate	prevent
on the grounds that	because
objective	aim
palpable	visible
proceed	go
reimburse	pay
salient	important
subsequent	next
take appropriate measures	act
terminate	end
utilize	use
within the realm of possibility	possible
wherewithal	means

Some of the flowery, elegant terms are actually shorter than their everyday equivalents, but length is not the most important criterion. Show-off words are free to anyone with a thesaurus, and they are seldom any more precise than the simpler forms. Your reader will feel more comfortable if you use familiar words.

SUMMARY

Flowery writing gives the impression of an attempt to show off the writer's intelligence. Unfortunately, it often has the opposite effect, and can make the writer look like a pompous fool. If there is a simpler, more familiar word, use it.

DISCUSS

1. Why would a person who when speaking would never think of showing off his or her intelligence use inflated language when writing?
2. Some elegant-sounding language may be as short as the everyday term. Why should you use the simpler word, even though most people will understand the more complex term?

ACT

Rewrite these sentences to put them in clear, simple language.
1. It is my considered opinion that those blessedly fortunate souls who manifest rare abilities in the faculties of hand-eye coordination should be eternally grateful to their ancestors rather than dame fortune.
2. The scribes who share the responsibility of recording important informational transactions in this learned establishment must also ground themselves in the ability to differentiate between extraneous and essential testimony.
3. It is within the realm of possibility that the salient features of your contract could be delineated, duly noted, and compensation directed to the party of the first part without benefit of legal counsel.

FOR YOUR JOURNAL

Student writers sometimes fall victim to elegant writing by trying to avoid repetition. When you find yourself using the same word over and over, you naturally want to add some variety.

A senior high school student, writing about her experiences applying to colleges, got concerned after the third time she used *college* in her introduction. *School* got her through the next paragraph, and then she made the mistake of looking in her thesaurus. By the time she started the fourth paragraph, she had treated her readers to *institutions of higher learning, professional training organizations,* and *endowed seats of learning.* If there were a rule to cover this, it would state that repetition is preferable to silliness.

A thesaurus is most useful if you know the word you're searching for but can't remember it. Used to find new ways to say the same thing, it's an invitation to disaster.

Take a page or two of your journal to show how avoiding repetition can sometimes lead to silliness. Pick a topic—Thanksgiving, your school's basketball team, your favorite make of car, anything at all. Then write about it, but use the actual name of your topic only once. After that, use a different pronoun or synonym every time you mention the topic. When you have finished, write one more paragraph describing how your nonrepetitious journal entry sounds.

Using Transitions

Once in a while, you look at an essay and realize that it hops and jumps, skipping from here to there without any logical connection between thoughts or paragraphs. Even though the paragraphs are about the same topic, the relationships are not clear; the ideas do not flow smoothly.

When this happens, look to your transitions. You need a bridge from one paragraph to the next or from one sentence to another. The easiest way to show relationships is to use the stepping-stones of transitional words and phrases. Each has its own purpose and can clarify relationships between sentences and paragraphs.

Relationship	Transitional Expressions
Addition	and, in addition, besides, then, too, also, another, just as important, not so obvious, first, second, again, next, last, as well as, finally, furthermore, beyond that

Example:
I have constant problems with math classes. *Another* problem area has been science.

Alternatives	or, either . . . or

Example:
Ilya could go to work for his father, *or* he may go to graduate school.

Concession	although, at least, though, even though, granted that, no doubt, of course

Example:
My small tape recorder works well for most purposes. *Of course,* Jerry's $75 model has better reproduction.

Condition	when, if

Example:
Samar wants to open her restaurant very soon. *When* all the necessary licenses are approved, that will be possible.

Contrast	on the other hand, but, however, in spite of, in contrast, still, yet, although, even though, on the contrary

Example:
The Ford has been a pretty good car, lasting through ten years of hard use. *On the other hand,* the Dodge is in questionable condition already.

Example	for example, for instance, to show, to illustrate, namely, especially, including, another

Example:
Drew has tried to prepare himself for a veterinary career. *For instance,* he worked at the humane society for three years.

Exclusion	neither . . . nor, all but, all except, but not

Example:
Practically everyone did well on the final test. *All but* Tom and John scored above 90 percent.

Purpose	in order to, so that, with this in mind

Example:
Hal wanted to meet Diane. *With this in mind,* he stood in the rain for an hour.

Result	so that, consequently, for this reason, as a result, therefore, so

Example:

Joe wrecked his car. *Consequently,* he has no way to get home for Easter.

Similarity   in the same way

Example:

Many of the women in our class are transferring into different majors. Rukku moved to the School of Business in her junior year and, *in the same way,* Tracy is making a change this year.

Words like these are directional signs that guide the reader from one sentence, paragraph, or idea to another. Leave these signs out and even well-thought-out essays can be difficult to follow. Use them carefully, and you link each idea to the one following it.

SUMMARY

Transitional words have two major functions in your essay. They direct the reader's thought from point to point, and they make clear the relationships among various parts of the essay. If your writing seems disjointed, as if you are randomly changing topics, check your transitions.

DISCUSS

1. Paragraphs are supposed to be self-sufficient structures. They should stand alone. Each has a topic sentence, a body, and a closing sentence. Why, then, do they need transitions to link them to other paragraphs?
2. Your essay should be unified in the sense that all of it, every paragraph and every sentence, supports the thesis. Why do you need transitions to link ideas in the essay?

ACT

For each of the following relationships, write two original sentences illustrating that relationship by using transitional words. Underline the transitional words.

Example:

Result: School will not dismiss until the second week of June this year. *Consequently,* we will find it even more difficult than usual to get summer jobs.

1. Addition
2. Alternatives
3. Concession
4. Conditional
5. Contrast
6. Example
7. Exclusion
8. Purpose
9. Result
10. Similarity

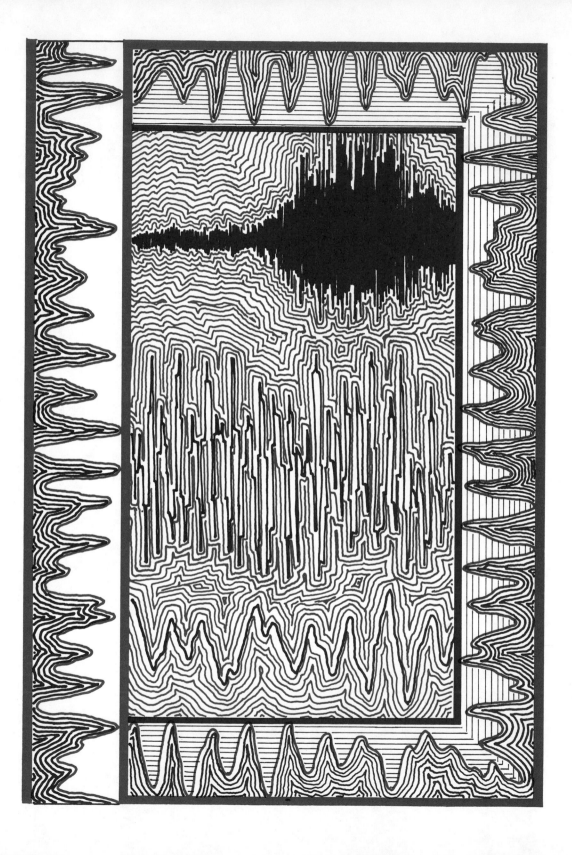

Finding Your Writing Voice

The way you talk makes you stand out from everyone else. There is a specialness about you that comes from a combination of influences: family, hometown, friends, school, reading, hobbies, memories, religion, dreams, and more. Any two of these are bound to make one person different from others, but the whole collection and the endless number of possible combinations mean that you are unique. And so, for that matter, is everyone else.

In spite of this, many people write stiff, unnatural sentences and paragraphs that look like they came out of a machine. As soon as these writers take pen in hand, they act like robots, lacking all individuality. They write stiffly because they have been told so often, by word and by example, that it is expected. Many writers have so thoroughly accepted the conventions of language that they actually feel uncomfortable being themselves, writing like they talk.

This does not mean that writing should be an imitation of speech. It's easy to live without "ya know," "uh," and "geez." What writing should be, though, is comfortable. It should sound like good conversation, even if it is a lot more trouble to get it down on paper.

When you read, you tend to form a picture of what the writer looks like. Lots of clues go into that visualization, but the main one is the way the person "talks." If he or she is stiff, artificial, and loaded with false dignity, you don't like the writer and turn off even good ideas. If the writer seems relaxed, confident, and secure, you are likely to listen sympathetically.

Be Yourself, Only Better

The challenge in writing is to picture yourself speaking to a friend. Get comfortable, and face that blank sheet of paper like a friend. Have the confidence to write in a way that is comfortable, quiet, simple, friendly. Don't try to impress your friend in writing any more than you would in person. Somewhere in that personal history of family, friends, school, and memories is a writing style of your own that can come out if you don't drown it in artificial language. Too often writers picture themselves as Fourth of July orators trying to drum up a vote. It doesn't work.

Maybe you don't believe that writing simply can lead to success. Perhaps you feel that overblown, pompous language is the sign of a learned person. Look around you. There is an endless supply of professional writers in print today. Look at some of the regular columnists in your daily newspaper: Mike Royko, Art Buchwald, Mary McGrory, Stephen Rosenfeld, David Broder, Flora Lewis—you know they are successful writers. Notice how simple their writing is. They don't need to impress anyone. They're already accepted as fine writers, and they got that way by turning out honest opinions and forgoing the opportunity to impress readers. Their only restriction is the belief that simplicity in language is a virtue. They express themselves with a force and dignity that is natural to native speakers of the language. You can, too. Use your own voice.

SUMMARY

Good writing is not impressive because it uses big words and artificial sentence structure. Good writing is impressive because it gives the impression of being relaxed, confident, and secure.

DISCUSS

1. What influences contribute to your uniqueness as a writer?
2. Why is it so difficult to write in a relaxed, confident, and secure manner?

ACT

Write two paragraphs on the topic of pompous, artificial writing. Make the wording as straightforward as possible. When you are finished, exchange papers with another student, and see if either of you can suggest further revisions.

Use Active Verbs

The active voice is just what you would expect—it emphasizes the doer of the action, and creates a greater sense of energy by putting the doer toward the beginning of the sentence. Because of this, it has a built-in directness that invigorates most writing. Given the choice, you should almost always use the active voice.

In the active voice, the subject of the sentence *performs* the action of the verb:

George punched John's lights out.

George is the doer in this sentence, and the active construction puts him right up front. The passive voice changes that crisp, lively sentence to an indirect, awkward one. In the passive voice, the subject of the sentence *receives* the action of the verb:

John's lights were punched out by George.

In spite of its awkwardness, the passive voice remains amazingly popular. It is certainly the object of much interest—at once feared by students, misunderstood by practically everyone, and overused by many people.

For some reason, the passive voice often sounds impressive. Because of this, many unsure people use the passive when there is no reason for it. Most of the time these writers are unaware of what is making their writing so dull and sluggish, and why it seems to take forever to explain the simplest idea.

For example, the passive voice says

A suggestion was made that a vote be taken, but the whole thing was postponed until the annual meeting could be called.

The active voice says

We postponed a vote until the annual meeting.

Most uses of the passive fall into one of four categories:

1. An occasional situation in which the passive is helpful
2. An attempt to introduce variety in a piece of writing

3. An unintentional use
4. An attempt to avoid giving information

Passive voice can sometimes be useful. For example, if you want to focus attention on the action itself or the thing being acted upon, passive voice names the receiver earlier in the sentence and may or may not name the performer.

> The state Capitol was destroyed (by the explosion).
> The Easter parade was ruined (by two hours of rain).
> The president may be impeached.

The passive voice is also helpful when you do not know who performed the action or do not wish to name that person.

> The equipment was stolen sometime last night. (The speaker doesn't know who stole the equipment and is spared having to say, "Some unknown person stole the equipment last night.")

> John has been elected secretary of his class. (No one wants to name all 216 people who voted for John.)

> Students should not be verbally abused that way. (To avoid embarrassment, the speaker would prefer to not name the guilty teacher.)

> Not all the essays will be done by this afternoon. (Again, the speaker would like to avoid embarrassment and awkwardness. "Some students, who shall remain nameless, will not have their essays done by this afternoon.")

The use of passive voice for variety's sake is common, and if you feel like occasionally using the passive, there is nothing wrong with it. On the other hand, accept the idea that accidental use will fill your quota early, and devote your energies to cutting it out.

Unintentional use, unfortunately, is the most common excuse. For this there is only one remedy. Recognize that too many passive verbs make your writing weak. Enliven your writing by sticking with the active.

Big problems arise when people discover that the passive voice makes it possible to sound as though you are giving a lot of information when you really aren't. For instance, the passive often pops up in government documents when bureaucrats try to avoid taking responsibility for their actions:

Mistakes were made in the tax law changes. (Who made the mistakes? We don't know.)

Social security recipients had their medical insurance dropped. (Who is responsible for this treatment of the elderly? We don't know.)

Bombs were dropped on the tiny island, and it was destroyed in minutes. (Who is responsible? Who ordered the bombing? We don't know.)

Poisonous chemicals were introduced into the drinking water of a Des Moines suburb today. (By now you get the idea. They don't want you to know who did it.)

This effect of withholding information seeps into even the most innocent writing. For instance, you may not have any reason to withhold information but, because of the passive construction, it seems that way. The best remedy is to avoid the passive voice.

The persistent use of active voice will do two good things for your writing: It will produce shorter, more direct sentences, and it will produce more lively sentences.

SUMMARY

Whenever possible, use the active voice. Passive voice should be considered only when you need to focus attention on the receiver of the action, or when you cannot name the performer of the action. Occasionally, the passive voice may provide variety.

DISCUSS

1. What is active voice? What is passive voice? Give an example of each.
2. Name two situations in which using the passive voice might improve your writing.
3. Why should the passive voice usually be avoided?

ACT

1. Rewrite the following passive sentences using the more direct active voice.
   a. The day Dad took us to the circus will always be remembered by me.
   b. An appointment can be made for you on the first Monday of the next month.
   c. The new seat belt law was explained by John Riley.
   d. Three visits were made by the building inspector.
2. The following sentences are written in the passive voice. Which ones should remain passive? Which should be reworded into active voice? Explain your decisions.
   a. Investigators fear that bribes are being made so that protection of the cocaine trade can be ensured.
   b. Monthly house payments will be adjusted as the interest rate is changed.
   c. Motorcycle helmets should be worn even on short trips.
   d. Mistreatment is being suffered by a high percentage of elderly residents of county facilities.
   e. The twelve-year-old was arraigned for the death of his two classmates.
   f. It was decided that this school will be closed permanently next year, and all students will be bused across town.
   g. Cancer was found in Mr. Target's lymph nodes.
   h. The sanitary conditions of our local restaurants are inspected almost monthly.

FOR YOUR JOURNAL

Americans are very conscious of their health. Most try to eat sensibly and keep fit. In fact, an entire industry has grown up around the physical fitness craze. People spend hundreds of dollars on running shoes and equipment, join health clubs where they lift weights, and attend aerobics classes that tone their muscles and improve their general fitness level.

Many experts recommend that people who take part in strenuous physical activity should spend some time doing stretching exercises both before and after. They should start, for example, with five minutes of various stretches to loosen muscles and prepare them for activity, and finish with another five minutes of stretching to relax the muscles after exercise. The stretching part of a physical fitness session can be an enjoyable and relaxing way to get into and out of the exercise.

People who are going to use their minds sometimes use mental stretching exercises to get themselves into and out of a creative session. Mental stretching can be anything from a little daydreaming to solving a difficult intellectual puzzle. One type of intellectual exercise has you devise creative solutions to a difficult problem.

For instance, pretend you are the sole beneficiary of your dear, departed Uncle Floyd's ceramic frog collection. Uncle Floyd spent a lifetime acquiring over 110,000 of the world's ugliest, most bizarre-looking, multicolored ceramic frogs. At the moment they are costing you $100 a month in storage fees. You need to turn this collection into an income producer that will cover your college expenses for the next four years. At the moment, no one is willing to purchase the frogs, so a direct sale is out of the question.

Use a couple of pages of your journal for this mental stretching exercise. Explain how you would use these frogs to put yourself through college. The only restriction is that you may not sell them. Be creative. Use your imagination.

Use Short, Varied Sentences

This may seem contrary to everything you have been taught, but your purpose in most writing is not to impress the reader with an elegant style. Your purpose is to communicate a message. To be sure you communicate that message clearly, make every effort to avoid two common pitfalls. First, don't confuse your reader with long, involved sentences that go on and on. Use some short sentences. Second, don't put the reader to sleep with long strings of short, overly simple sentences that would insult the intelligence of an eighth-grade comic book reader. Use some variety.

Variety has no absolute rules. There are hundreds of ways to achieve it, and at least another hundred ways of going wrong. Long strings of very short sentences can start to sound sing-songy. At the very least, they sound childish. Moreover, a series of simple sentences connected by *and, and,* and *and* is equally tiresome.

The greatest difficulty for most people, however, is those long, long sentences. Short, choppy sentences can seem simple-minded, but very long ones are worse and seem to occur more often. If you must err, err on the side of the short and simple.

It's not easy to know how long is too long or how short is too short. There really aren't any rules, but variety is the important element.

In any piece of writing, several sentences deserve special attention: The first and last sentences, the thesis sentence, and the first and last sentences of each paragraph.

If you write a paragraph that contains several very short sentences, play with the words a little and try to put the first two or three sentences together. Try the same thing with the last few sentences. If the paragraph consists of five or six long sentences, write short, punchy, contrasting sentences for the important positions. Whatever the situation, try to avoid monotony.

The following paragraph could use a little variety.

> The fact that we used to limit women to a few narrow opportunities does not mean that these opportunities are any less demanding, responsible, fulfilling, or worthwhile. Although we have done a fair job of making the traditional men's positions available to some women, we have done nothing about making traditional women's positions more prestigious, more lucrative to the most talented of either sex. On the contrary, we have systematically devalued those tasks to which women have been confined, not because of the nature of the task, but because of our mistaken attitudes toward women.

The paragraph consists of three sentences (that's no problem) with 27, 37, and 31 words, respectively (that's a problem!). The paragraph reads better if you add a couple of short sentences to the beginning and end.

> Remember women's work? The fact that we used to limit women to a few narrow opportunities does not mean that these opportunities are any less demanding, responsible, fulfilling, or worthwhile. Although we have done a fair job of making the traditional men's positions available to some women, we have done nothing about making traditional women's positions more prestigious and lucrative to the most talented of either sex. On the contrary, we have systematically devalued those tasks to which women have been confined. That's not because of the nature of the task but

because of our attitudes toward women. The mistake may come back to haunt us.

That paragraph feels a lot better. If those changes are still not enough, break up one of the middle sentences. Never hesitate to use a period. In fact, by this time you shouldn't be stopped by the old admonition against starting a sentence with *and, or,* or *but.* The sentence in the middle of that paragraph easily becomes, "We have done a fair job of making the traditional men's positions available to some women. But we have done nothing about making traditional women's positions more prestigious and lucrative to the most talented of either sex." You may be breaking someone's pet rule, but the improvement is worth it.

The average sentence length should be around twenty words. More important than that twenty-word suggestion, though, is the fact that those sentences run anywhere from a low of four or five words up to thirty and more words. There is no absolute standard to follow, but some examples might help.

Look back at the first paragraph of this section on page 68. That paragraph has seven sentences using all kinds of sentence structures. Count the words in each sentence and write the totals in your journal. What's the longest sentence? What's the shortest? Some paragraphs will show more variety than that, and some will show a lot less, but the idea is that readers should not see a lot of repetition.

If that first paragraph were written entirely in seven-word sentences, it would sound silly and the meanings would be blurred. Take a look.

You get a lot of writing advice. This is going to seem very different. College writing doesn't have just one purpose. You could impress the reader with elegance. It is better to communicate a message. You should avoid two very common mistakes. Don't use too many long, involved sentences. Don't use too many short, choppy sentences. Use short sentences, and use some variety.

Not only is the above paragraph ridiculous, but it has lost a good deal of meaning.

Even if you don't feel comfortable with grammatical terms, even if you have trouble remembering the difference between a simple, compound, or complex sentence (not to mention a compound-complex sentence), you can achieve variety by using different sentence structures. See how many ways you can write the same sentence. Ten different possibilities are not unusual. Five should be possible for most sentences. See if you can add several more possibilities to those examples.

> Women who would like to take a course in self-defense should consider two new ones being offered next semester.
> If you want to learn self-defense, think about these new courses for next semester.
> A lot of students would benefit from lessons in self-defense, and the P. E. department is offering two new courses soon.
> If you want to learn self-defense, you may be interested in these two courses, and you'll have the chance to take one next semester.

These sentences say nearly the same thing, but they do so in different ways and give a little different sound and feeling to the message each time the wording changes. If you want to break the original sentence into two sentences, even more variety is possible:

> Want to learn self-defense? Look at these courses being offered next semester.

You only need one great way to say it, and what is great depends on how it sounds in context—the place you use it.

SUMMARY

The thesis sentence, the first and last sentences of each paragraph, and the first and last sentences of your paper all deserve special attention. Your sentences will probably average about twenty words, but more important, sentences should vary from a few words to thirty or more. The types of sentence structures you use should be as varied as possible.

DISCUSS

1. Why should you avoid writing a series of long sentences?
2. Short sentences can also be a problem. Why?

ACT !!

1. Rewrite each of the following sentences. You should be able to create at least two improved versions of each, but be sure to retain the meaning while creating a variety of structures.
   a. The mayor's renewed interest in balancing the budget is attributable to practical political considerations.
   b. Any expansion of a government-sponsored health program will probably run into a great deal of opposition from members of the American Medical Association.
   c. The student who spends his or her high school years taking a series of courses designed to guarantee a four-point GPA is doomed to emerge an uneducated graduate.
   d. All of my writing seems to be criticized for one of two things; either I get accused of triteness, or the teachers cannot see the basic organizational structure I had in mind.

2. Rewrite this paragraph changing some tiresomely long sentences into shorter, more interesting ones.

   The lawn was really quite a mess with its broken weeping willow trees scattered from front to back. More often than not, you could see the children's toys strewn all over the place, some even hanging where they had been left in the trees. The brown grass was only spotty, and sand and rocks made mowing the lawn even more of an unpleasant chore than you might have imagined at first. Just to make the job even more of a challenge, the children continued to race back and forth in front of the mower, making a game out of dodging it at the last minute. I finally told Mrs. Armbruster that I would have to turn down the job if she couldn't pay more than five dollars for what turned out to be a three-hour chore.

3. Rewrite the following paragraph varying the sentence length. Try to avoid the choppy effect.

   Jenny bought a computer. It was a well known brand. The price was low. She charged it. She types on it. It corrects her spelling. Her grades have improved.

FOR YOUR JOURNAL

People are always making lists: lists of groceries to buy, lists of things to do, lists of assignments to complete. Lists are popular because they provide an effective way for people to organize their activities.

Even this book contains a lot of lists. Most of them are intended to help you get your thoughts together, or organize your writing skills.

The trouble with lists is that you begin to resent them. Much like having too many rules to remember, every one of them feels like one more demand on you and your time. The fact that they actually make the task easier doesn't change the perception that lists are demanding.

Once in a while it feels good to revolt. For a few minutes, use your journal to contradict the lists of writing suggestions you see so often. Make up your own list of a dozen rules a student should follow in order to write a failing essay. Use your imagination. You might even practice some of your own rules as you write them.

1. Don't be overly concerned with your speling.
2. By the age of seventeen, misplaced modifiers should not be causing you any concern.
3. The use of foreign words and phrases is de rigueur.

Remember Your Readers

A good salesperson makes it a habit to learn as much as possible about a new prospect. Every scrap of information is useful: interests, abilities, hobbies, income, marital status—they all help. And when the salesperson approaches the prospect, he or she does it with a personalized plan that takes into account the needs and desires of a real human being, not some generic customer.

A good salesperson would use totally different approaches for a farmer and for a stockbroker. They have very different points of view and interests. The great salesperson will even use different approaches on a small farmer and a large farmer, an Iowa hog farmer and an Arkansas tomato farmer, a Kansas wheat farmer and an Illinois corn farmer. That salesperson knows the client he or she is talking to and adjusts the sales talk accordingly.

Knowing your customer is just as appropriate in writing. Know the person you are writing for. Don't write a paper for a humanities class; write a paper for Ms. Higgins or Mr. Baca or whoever. Write it for an individual and adjust your emphasis accordingly.

This does not mean that you should disguise your beliefs to conform to those of your reader. Some politicians have been caught doing that, and it is just as dishonest if you do it. Don't feed Mr. Swallow ideas you think he will approve of. It won't be authentic, and unless he is a complete fool, he'll catch on fast anyway.

Do keep in mind, however, what life is like for this forty-two-year-old high school teacher on the day he gets around to reading your paper. He has spent the better part of it standing in front of five different classes. Many of his students were less interested than they should have been. He is tired. His son's college tuition is due, and his daughter is still dating that unemployed moron. He promised your papers would be returned by Friday; it's 11 p.m. Thursday, and so far every paper has been dull, dull, dull.

Please don't write what you think he wants to hear. Everybody else is already doing that. He's not in the mood for more. What will really please him is a two or three-page paper that he can read and understand in five to ten minutes. Nothing fancy. Nothing literary. Just good old straightforward American English. Knowing immediately what your purpose is and why you think it's important would make his day. Get it said, explain yourself, and let the poor man go to bed. He will reward you.

Maybe that doesn't sound like your teacher. Maybe she is twenty-five, single, and rides home on a Kawasaki. Maybe that's all you know about her. Fine. Whatever you can tell about your reader's age, sex, education, interests, and life's experiences is going to help—anything so you can get over thinking of her as a faceless mass and yourself as standing at a lectern preaching.

Try the bathroom mirror trick. While you're brushing your hair or shaving in the morning, talk to this person. Phrase your argument a few different ways. Carry on an imaginary conversation. Try out the sound of your words and use this time to get them just right. Then sit down and write it out while the words are still fresh and conversational in your mind.

Another trick that helps a lot of writers is to role-play the intended reader. Granted, it's difficult to accurately cast yourself as someone else, to take on the attitudes of that person. But the results are worth it. How would you feel about your paper if you had never seen it before? Set it aside for awhile.

Now, how does it look? Try to sense the attitude of the reader. Have you left out any key information? Sometimes information and ideas are so obvious that explanations seem unnecessary. Unfortunately, they may be obvious only to the writer. Now that you are the reader, is there any reason you should be expected to know all this background information?

"Everybody knows that" is not a valid response. Maybe only Joe Student knows that. If there's any chance your reader needs the information, give it to her. She won't resent the simplification, and as long as you don't start sounding like a third-grade reading book, she'll be appreciative.

The good salesperson always writes for the individual. Talk to that person, get the words down on paper, and role-play the audience to see how your ideas look from the reader's point of view. Try it in every class you write for. Nobody minds being able to read faster, understand better, and enjoy more.

SUMMARY

Direct your writing to a specific reader. Picture yourself speaking to that person, and select your information and wording with that individual's background, interests, and concerns in mind.

DISCUSS

1. Why is it important to picture your audience?
2. Describe two methods you can use to be more certain you will communicate well with your reader.

ACT

List three assumptions you could make about your audience in each of these situations.

1. You are writing to the mayor of your city about a proposed change in the zoning laws.
2. You are writing to the board of education about your school's graduation requirements.
3. You are writing a letter to the editor of a newspaper with statewide circulation.
4. You are writing a letter to apply for a scholarship at your state university.
5. You are writing a social studies report that will be read before the whole class.
6. You are writing a speech to be given at your high school commencement.

7. You are writing an antismoking essay directed at your class-mates.
8. You are writing an antismoking essay directed at the fathers of young children.
9. You are writing an antismoking essay directed at pregnant women.
10. You are writing an antismoking essay directed at a senior citizens group.

Checklist for Writers

If you follow these guidelines, you should have an impressive-looking final copy. The suggestions assume a typewritten copy, but most will also apply to handwritten work. If the assignment cannot be typed, at least use black ink.

1. Always use good-quality, white paper. Erasable bond paper creates a mess. Instead, get a bottle of correction fluid for errors.
2. Leave generous margins. Minimums are one and one-half inches at the left, top, and bottom of each page, with no less than an inch on the right.
3. Use only one side of each sheet of paper.
4. In the upper left-hand corner of page 1, inside the margins, put your name, the date, the course, and any other appropriate information, such as the teacher's name and the specific assignment. Each item goes on a separate line, single-spaced.
5. Double-space the rest of the assignment.
6. Center the title no more than one-third of the way down page 1. Don't use quotation marks.
7. After the title, skip four spaces and begin the first paragraph.
8. Indent the first lines of each paragraph five spaces. If you are writing by hand, indent at least one-half inch.
9. Starting on page 2, number each page either at the bottom or in the upper right-hand corner. Unless the teacher gives different instructions, staple pages in the upper left-hand corner.

10. Short quotations should be enclosed in quotation marks. When a quotation is at least two sentences and four or five lines long, it can be indented five to ten spaces on both the left and right margins. Single space quotes of this type.

Here's the beginning of a student paper that shows a typical format:

Amy Austin
Composition II
Ms. Chung
March 12, 19 _____

Where's the Support?

The cool silence of the gym is disturbed only by the monotonous thudding of a basketball being dribbled down the court and an occasional "Go Tigers" screamed from a bench-warming team-mate. Clad in her ragged uniform of faded red polyester, the leading scorer goes up for the basket that will bring victory in the final seconds of a very close game. The swish of the basket as the ball passes through it is drowned out by the game-ending buzzer. It's over! They've won against incredible odds. But instead of the thunderous roar of adoring fans, only a half-hearted "Good game" from the opposing team's captain is heard by the girls' basketball team as they file off the court. This is an all-too-familiar scene at Cedar Falls High School. Not only girls' basketball is affected by this lack of support; all girls' sports and activities, such as cheerleading and pom-pom squads, are overshadowed by our school's emphasis on male sports. The administration should stop spotlighting boys' athletics, and spend more time and money on girls' activities.

5

Cause and Effect

Ever since a man named Grog stepped out of his cave to check the weather and was struck by a stray bolt of lightning 40,000 years ago, humans have been trying to piece together cause-and-effect explanations for what happens to them. In Grog's case, his neighbors conducted a less-than-exhaustive inquiry and concluded that the gods were angry about Grog's failure to help gather firewood the night before.

More recently, and more scientifically, Americans searched for a cause behind the spacecraft *Challenger* disaster in which social studies teacher Christa McAuliffe and six other astronauts were killed. In the *Challenger* disaster, NASA scientists and engineers concluded that an O-ring failed to seal, causing a leakage of hot gases that led to the fatal explosion.

On a more personal level, you or a friend may have tried recently to discover the cause behind an unexpectedly low grade or a car that wouldn't start in the morning. Your attempts to uncover the causes behind such events mean that you use cause-effect reasoning without consciously deciding to do so. Cause-and-effect is not just an artificial method of organizing your writing but a pattern of reasoning that you will use throughout your life.

A Real-life Application

Harold Martin, mayor of a midsized Iowa city, found this to be true when he ran into a difficult problem. The city's streets had been deteriorating for years, and there was no money to step up the street repair program. Considering its budget, the street department was well run. The administration was constantly working for greater efficiency, and the employees were conscientious and hardworking. They just needed more money.

Over the last few years the city's income had been reduced because of a declining tax base. A major employer in the area laid off assembly-line workers, and hundreds of families moved away to look for jobs elsewhere. What was a minor recession nationally became an overwhelming depression in Sturgis Falls.

The mayor decided to ask the voters to approve a temporary 1 percent sales-tax increase. This would be a local tax added to the present 4 percent state sales tax. He knew that the best he could hope for was a fair hearing for his idea because citizens would be reluctant to add to their tax burden. As if that weren't enough, no member of the city council wanted to be associated with raising taxes. The mayor spent weeks planning his presentation to the city council and the news media. When the big day arrived, Harold Martin had his arguments prepared.

First, he stated the causes for his request. The streets were in abysmal shape, both in residential areas and near the city's industrial section. Potholes reappeared with each spring thaw. Main Street had become an obstacle course. Several traffic accidents were directly attributable to street conditions, and the city could be held liable.

Two years earlier the town's main employer, Arco International, laid off 650 workers, resulting in a loss thus far of two hundred families. With the national recession, there was a general decline in income, and the economic climate showed no signs of improvement. As time went on, the city streets were bound to get worse. The city's chances of gaining new industry seemed less and less likely. Several out-of-town industry representatives who had inquired about locating in Sturgis Falls commented that the city's transportation problem played a part in their decision to go elsewhere. City leaders should expect that no one would want to locate new industry there until the streets were improved. One small employer actually left town in the last six months, saying that problems involving delivery of materials played a part in his decision.

Meanwhile it cost a great deal each year just to keep patching the old streets. It would cost more, of course, to completely repave most of the streets, but patching and repatching seemed to be costing more than they were worth, considering the fact that the streets never did really improve all that much.

In the second part of his presentation, the mayor discussed the effects of the temporary 1 percent sales tax. With it the city would be able, within the next eighteen months, to repave 45 percent of the town's major streets. On Main Street, traffic would be able to move smoothly again. The town probably could retain all of its present industry and stood a good chance of attracting two new employers with the promise of better, safer routes for trucks. When the employment outlook in town improved, city fathers could expect increased property values, and the temporary sales tax should no longer be necessary. Certainly, within three or four years, the city would be able to return to a more traditional method of maintaining the streets. Citizens would save money on the upkeep of their cars, and the overall result could even be a savings.

Although the mayor's argument was presented orally, he did have it written out, and it did contain a thesis: "The voters should approve this request for a temporary, 1 percent sales tax to be used for improving the city's streets." He then went on to support that thesis with his subpoints, all of which depended on cause-effect reasoning.

You have probably noticed that the terms *cause* and *effect*, as used in the mayor's speech, are somewhat relative. An effect can become the cause of another effect. Some of the causes the mayor talked about could also be viewed as the effects of a decline in municipal income (less money led to more potholes, more potholes led to more accidents, more accidents led to additional city liability). In addition, some of the effects could be viewed as causing industry to return to Sturgis Falls (New paving is an effect of the 1 percent sales tax, but it is also a cause of employment being attracted to the city.) Whether a situation is considered a cause or an effect depends a great deal on your point of view. The resulting chain of events can be very involved, but it is not likely to cause problems as long as you remain aware of how any given cause or effect is functioning in its relationship to the rest of the essay.

In Harold Martin's case, the presentation was so clear and convincing that the interrelationships only served to make his argument more effective. He got his 1 percent tax, and Sturgis Falls began a revitilization project that continues even today. Although it took five years, the city was soon able to rescind the tax and continue its street program without the extra revenue.

SUMMARY

People constantly use cause-effect reasoning without being aware of the process. It is a normal thought pattern as well as a method of organizing your writing. Sometimes, an effect that follows a cause can become the impetus for another event, starting a long string of related causes and effects. Whether a situation is considered a cause or an effect depends a great deal on your point of view.

DISCUSS

1. Why is cause-and-effect reasoning so common in human experience?
2. What practical purposes are served by knowing why events occurred or what effects can be expected to follow from some action?

ACT

1. Write one paragraph describing a news event for which people have tried to find a cause.
2. Write a second paragraph describing those causes. If causes have been identified, what are they? Do they seem believable? Explain. If causes have not yet been found, what are some likely possibilities?
3. Write one paragraph describing a current situation for which people have tried to determine what effects can be expected.
4. Write a second paragraph describing the effects those people expect.

FOR YOUR JOURNAL

In the first half of this century, divorce was quite uncommon and carried a definite stigma. Most states made obtaining a divorce very difficult by requiring that either the husband or wife prove sufficient grounds. Typical grounds were adultery, desertion, habitual drunkenness, conviction of a felony, or "cruel and inhuman treatment."

Some states, however, made divorce much easier. In the early 1900s, the Nevada legislature changed the state's residency requirements for divorce. People could obtain a divorce six months after moving there. Within months hotels, restaurants, and casinos were flourishing. Later, the residency requirement was lowered to six weeks. Those who could afford it would, for example, spend six weeks vacationing in Nevada and come home with a tan and a divorce.

Today most states have changed their laws so that people who want to divorce may do so without having to move. Neither the husband nor the wife has to prove that the other has done something terrible. If either, or both, of them wants out, it is fairly easy.

In recent years various sources have estimated that between one in three and one in two marriages end in divorce. Some people see a direct cause-and-effect relationship between the ease of getting divorced and the high divorce rate. Others think it's not that simple. They say the divorce rate is only one of the effects of a large number of social changes. These changes include increased acceptance of divorce, more financial independence for women, and even people being more demanding in what they think is an acceptable state of marriage. If a husband or wife is not happy, he or she will divorce in order to seek out a better marriage.

What do you think are the major causes of today's high divorce rate? In your journal, write down your thoughts on the causes and effects of divorce in the United States. Try to take a broad view. What causes divorce, and what effects come from divorce? How does it affect the family, the schools, the country?

Four Guides to Basic Organization

When you're developing a cause-effect argument, you'll make the job a lot easier if you follow four simple steps.

Examine All Possible Causes or Effects

Do not oversimplify. Don't assume that any event is the result of a single cause or that any cause will result in only one effect.

You've probably seen people fixated on one cause while trying to figure out why something happened. As a result, they overlooked more significant causes.

For example, it is common for athletic teams to give all the credit or blame to one player for the team's win-loss record. It's not unusual for a quarterback to gather most of the praise for what is actually a team effort or for one particularly good basketball player to receive all the acclaim from sportswriters when the credit for success belongs to the whole team. Although one player may be very important, he or she could not win the games—or lose them—alone.

In another example, a Midwestern high school had a particularly ineffective student forum. Many students, looking for the causes of the problem, realized that the president of the forum was not much of a leader. She had been elected in a year when the competition was not great and became president almost by default.

Unfortunately, once the students focused on that one cause, they forgot to look for others and, in reality, the president was not the cause of all the problems. She was only one factor, only one weak link in a chain of weak links. Among other problems, the forum faculty sponsor had been ill a great deal that year and had missed many meetings. In addition, the representatives weren't taking their responsibilities seriously, and many of them were not reporting back to their homerooms regularly. Consequently, few students in the school were aware of what the forum really was or was not doing.

In your own cause-effect reasoning, be careful not to oversimplify and overlook other significant factors. It is better to begin by brainstorming as many ideas as you can possibly come up with. Don't be concerned about whether some seem trivial. Just make a list of as many different causes or effects as you can. Make sure you give yourself time at the beginning to think of all the possibilities that could enter into the situation. Later, if it becomes obvious that, out of the ten or fifteen ideas, some are unimportant, you can always narrow the list to four or five of the best.

Look For Relationships

Do not overlook links in a chain of events. There may be many intermediate steps connecting what looks like a simple cause-effect relationship. For instance, an increase in divorce may lead to more juvenile crime, but there are many intermediate, related steps, and any possible connection between divorce and crime is not as direct and easy to follow as you may at first think. Divorce leads to single-parent families, and that usually leads to lower income. Lower income might well lead to the custodial parent being employed and out of the home eight or ten hours a day. That could lead to inadequate supervision of the children, and inadequate supervision could lead to the opportunity for juvenile crime.

Notice that every one of these steps is only a possibility, not a certainty. Each one of them is fully dependent on all the causes before it, and each one of them is going to require an explanation if you are writing about the subject. Unless you carefully support each step in the chain, your reader may have trouble following your line of thought.

Distinguish Degrees of Importance

A third step in writing your cause-and-effect essay is to identify the most significant of all the possible causes and effects that you've listed. In a 500-to-750 word paper, you aren't going to have space to fully treat every possible cause. You have brainstormed all the possibilities so that you wouldn't overlook anything important, but some of them will be more important than others. Take the three or four most important causes or effects, and discuss them fully. Give each a well-developed paragraph.

If, in the final draft, you give space to insignificant information, it will look as though you're stretching to prove your point, that you don't have anything better to use as an explanation. If you can't develop an idea fully and show its significance, either drop it entirely or mention it in such a way that you make clear you are aware of it and believe it is not too unimportant.

For example, in the case of the ineffective student forum, when people made a list of all the causes involved, they remembered that the forum meeting room was unattractive and needed remodeling. Compared to some of the other reasons, that one was insignificant, but the fact that the students insisted on including it in their explanation gave the impression that they felt it was important. It hurt the credibility of the people who were trying to explain how the problems of the student forum went beyond the president's inadequacies.

Organize Your Essay

If your causes or effects are linked together in a time sequence, your decision is already made, and you should present them chronologically. Usually, though, the question of how to organize a paper is not answered that easily.

Most often, you are going to have to rank the most significant ideas in order of importance. You need to rank them for one major reason—you have to present your essay in an order that your reader can follow. One of your causes is going to have to come first; one is going to come last. It is not possible to say that the most important idea should always come first or that the most important should always come last. Sometimes, the first position will be most effective; sometimes the last position might seem the best place to put your most important idea.

The main thing to remember is that you should present your ideas in a logical fashion, not just in any old order. Have a reason why you put each idea where you put it. You don't need to explain that reason to your reader, but you should have thought it through so that your essay can be as easy to follow and as convincing as possible.

SUMMARY

Start by making a list of all possible causes or effects, checking closely for any relationships between them. Don't overlook any possible links in a chain of events. Distinguish between degrees of importance, and organize your essay in a deliberate fashion.

DISCUSS

1. In what way can oversimplifying causes or effects be dangerous?
2. What process can you use to avoid oversimplification?
3. One of the steps for developing cause-effect arguments involves looking for additional relationships between causes and effects. Beyond the simple "event 1 caused event 2," what kinds of relationships should you expect to find?
4. Why should you distinguish degrees of importance when planning your presentation?

ACT

1. Consider the following as effects. Choose three and list six possible causes of each.
   a. The American Revolution
   b. A broad knowledge of current events
   c. A winning athletic team
   d. The high cost of quality audio systems
   e. The high cost of insurance for young drivers

2. Consider the following as causes. Choose three and list six possible effects of each.
   a. Rush-hour traffic jams
   b. Injuries at a rock concert
   c. Corrupt city government
   d. Springtime floods
   e. Speeding in a school zone
3. Choose one of the cause-effect relationships you identified above. Rank your six causes or effects and write a six-to-ten-sentence paragraph explaining why you put them in that order. Be sure to explain why you consider each to be more or less important than the others.

Three Traps to Avoid

In writing your essay, there are some pitfalls to avoid when detailing cause and effect.

Don't Confuse Time with Cause or Effect

Sometimes, events will take place one right after the other. Because the second event follows on the heels of the first, it may seem as if they are related, as if the first event caused the second. This is not necessarily the case. You must find a true, causal relationship.

For example, imagine yourself sitting in math class, listening to Ms. Lee explain a difficult concept. Except for the sound of her voice, the classroom is quiet, and the students are all busily taking notes. Ms. Lee, her back to the class, is putting figures on the chalkboard when all of a sudden a wastebasket comes flying through the open door, bounces over the top of her desk, and scatters its contents across the front of the room. Ms. Lee runs to the hallway but sees only a stairwell door slamming shut at the end of the hall.

Knowing it is too late to catch the culprit, she walks to the window, and a few seconds later sees Bruce Presgrave run out the front door, sprint across the lawn, and jump into a waiting van which then speeds away.

Does the time relationship—the thrown wastebasket followed almost immediately by Bruce Presgrave's hasty departure—mean that Bruce is the guilty party?

If your answer is yes, maybe you should think again. Whoever threw the wastebasket could have run in several directions. Possibly the person did run directly into the stairwell. At the bottom of the stairs, the culprit once again could have gone in several different directions. You don't know that he or she ran through the front door of the school and into the van. Consider also that the boy Ms. Lee saw could have come from many places in the school. He could have been doing all sorts of things while the basket was being thrown. He could have been coming from the principal's office, or he could have been coming from the guidance office. There are many reasons he might have been leaving the building at that time. The fact that Ms. Lee saw him run out of the building almost immediately after the incident does not, in itself, mean that he was guilty of anything.

At the same time, however, it is evidence. In putting together a case to figure out who did throw the wastebasket, it would be silly to ignore the fact that Bruce was observed running from the building. But Ms. Lee has to remember that it is just that—evidence. It is only one fact, which might or might not contribute to identifying the guilty person.

Don't Mistake Symptoms for Causes

Events almost never occur in isolation. If your father is cooking supper in an electric frying pan, for example, and the electricity suddenly goes off, he might ask you to check whether a fuse has blown. If, in fact, the fuse serving that part of the house has blown, the first thing you would do is replace it. If that solves the problem, the story is over.

But what if the following day the same fuse were to blow at about the same time? You would probably find the blown fuse and replace it again. It might occur to you that simply replacing the fuse the day before didn't actually solve the problem. What you did was treat the symptom of a larger problem. Perhaps your father's frying pan has a short in it which is causing too large a draw on your house's wiring system. Perhaps there is something deficient in the wiring of your kitchen. There could be any number of causes behind the effect you are seeing, and the blown fuse is only a symptom of some greater problem.

To take a different example, say you are studying a Third World country that is losing thousands of people to famine. The first cause of that country's problems may appear to be starving people, or, going back a step, an inadequate agricultural system. But possibly these are just symptoms of an even more basic problem. Is it possible that the country's problems could stem from its economic or political systems?

You need to consider the possibility that the agricultural problems, the food-distribution problems, and the starving people are symptoms of something much bigger; and while you want to help those people, simply feeding them may not get at the ultimate cause of the situation. It's entirely possible that you may find yourself in the trap of mistaking symptoms for causes.

Foresee False Causes and Effects

You can make your essay more convincing by anticipating and answering objections your reader may raise. A reader will take your arguments more seriously if you show why those objections are not valid.

If your car won't start in the morning and you're trying to figure out what has to be done to get it running again, you need to determine exactly what the problem is. There are several possible causes; mentally you make a list of them. You may have a list of ten or twelve items. It would help greatly if you knew from the beginning that some definitely did not play a part in the problem. You could rule them out without having to test each one. The same holds true in your essay. Your reader may have several objections that you can eliminate right from the beginning by showing the reader that these possible causes do not play a part. You can narrow the possibilities very quickly.

On the other hand, if your reader has specific ideas in mind and you don't mention them, your reader may decide that you never considered those possibilities and that you don't really understand the situation. In the reader's mind, you are overlooking obvious causes behind the problem you are attempting to discuss.

In reality, you may have considered them and dismissed them, but the reader doesn't know that unless you mention them and explain why you can't take those causes seriously.

SUMMARY

When thinking through your cause-and-effect essay, be careful not to confuse time order with a cause-effect relationship. Also, be aware of the possibility that what looks like a cause may be no more than an additional effect of the cause you are trying to explain. Finally, watch for the possibility that false causes or effects may mislead your reader.

DISCUSS

1. How can time order confuse the search for causes?
2. Explain the difference between symptoms and causes. Include at least one example of your own.
3. What is the advantage of identifying false causes or effects early in your explanation?

ACT

!!

Look at each of the following effects. On a sheet of paper, label each possible cause as a probable cause or as only a symptom. In one or two sentences, explain your choices.

1. *Effect:* Our football team had a poor season.
   Possible causes:
   - a. Our quarterbacks suffered serious injuries.
   - b. The team lost its first three games.
   - c. The new coach's system was difficult to learn.
   - d. Fan support grew worse with each game.
   - e. The team was eliminated in the first postseason tournament game.
2. *Effect:* Central High School students are success-oriented.
   Possible causes:
   - a. Nearly every student is taking at least five subjects.
   - b. Science, math, and writing courses are overloaded every semester.
   - c. The honor society is one of the most active in the state.
   - d. Seventy-five percent go on to college.
   - e. Twenty-five percent go to professional schools after earning undergraduate college degrees.

FOR YOUR JOURNAL

People approach unpleasant tasks with all sorts of methods. Some operate on the principle that since being done with the job is so pleasant they will begin immediately. Others procrastinate.

Almost everyone has suffered from procrastination, from putting off some unpleasant task that should be done. Some people make an art of it. In fact, many seem to take great pride in their avoidance techniques. They make up humorous rules—"Don't put off until tomorrow what you can get done sometime next week"—and even form organizations. One national procrastinator's club conducts its annual meetings exactly one year late—the 1988 meeting, for example, was held in 1989.

The problem is that procrastination isn't always humorous. Maybe you have heard horror stories about someone who puts off balancing the checkbook or paying bills. There is nothing humorous about receiving a collection notice from a department store, or having the telephone service cut off or your car repossessed.

One man spent a night in jail because he put off paying, and then forgot about several parking tickets. By the time the legal system got around to him, five $3.00 parking tickets, plus penalties, interest, court costs, and collection fees, had grown to $177. When he could not produce enough cash (no checks for scofflaws), he was taken into custody on a contempt of court charge. The next day his wife was able to gather the necessary cash. The newspaper article did not mention how the man explained being late for his job that day.

Not all procrastination leads to these extreme results, but most people learn, somewhere along the way, that putting off until tomorrow can be dangerous. What kinds of responsibilities do you, or your friends and family, have that need to be done according to some schedule?

In your journal, explain what these responsibilities are and what the consequences might be if the job is not done. Try to include procrastination that might have long-term effects, perhaps reaching years into the future.

The Parts and the Whole

Before considering an entire essay using cause-and-effect relationships, two important features deserve to be illustrated and explained.

Introductions

Any method of introduction you have learned can be used in a cause-effect essay, but some specialized approaches may be especially appropriate.

A cause-effect paper can be either a prediction of what will happen if a particular set of events occurs, or an explanation of why something happened in the past.

If you are writing a paper that explains why something happened, it may be a good idea to introduce your essay with some background information and a summary of effects you have observed. For example, if you are writing about the causes of price gouging by gasoline retailers in your city, you might introduce the essay this way:

> On March 24, 1989, Good Friday of that year, the 987-foot-long *Exxon Valdez* plowed into a reef south of Valdez, Alaska. The supertanker dumped 240,000 barrels of crude oil into Prince William Sound, and, in less than a week, the oil covered nine hundred square miles of water. A shocked world looked on as Exxon first tried to escape its responsibility and then bungled attempts at a cleanup. For several weeks Exxon, Prince William Sound, and the massive oil spill were on front pages everywhere. No one was surprised when the price of gasoline began to edge up, a few cents at a time, and continued to climb until it had increased by a full twenty-five cents a gallon at the station in my neighborhood. Considering the fact that the 240,000-barrel spill was a tiny percentage of the oil used in this country, the increased prices seemed unreasonable. The high prices of fuel products in April and May of 1989 were a result of oil companies taking advantage of and dramatizing a nonexistent shortage.

From this point you would go on to explain the various causes behind the high prices of fuel.

On the other hand, if you are writing a paper that shows effects, it would be a good idea to introduce the essay by reviewing the causes. For example, if you are writing about the effects of a dangerous dependence on a single industry in your town, you might open your essay in this manner:

> Ridgewood, Alabama, depends entirely too much on its one big employer, the J. D. Oleson Manufacturing Company. Over 16,000 men

and women are employed full or part-time. Another 2,500 workers are involved with industries that depend on Oleson Manufacturing for their sales. For example, Allen Steel Company sells raw materials to the giant factory, and Derek Catering serves lunches to three shifts of workers six days a week. In all, more than 70 percent of the Ridgewood population depends on the financial well-being of J. D. Oleson. Right now, with a healthy economy, that seems to be a pleasant arrangement, but we cannot count on our good fortune continuing forever. If, or when, the economy takes a turn for the worse, and Oleson Manufacturing has to begin laying off workers, Ridgewood will suffer a massive depression.

In the body of your paper, you would explain the specific effects the city could expect to suffer.

Transitions

Use transitions carefully as signposts to help your reader follow your logical pattern of reasoning from cause to effect or from effect to cause.

Examples:

Another effect of Post-Vietnam Stress Disorder is . . .

A *secondary* cause behind President Bush's decision was . . .

Hence, the major reason for the disaster at Chernoble was a lack of basic safety rules.

As a consequence, the police department is understaffed.

For this reason, we must be careful to avoid any hint of wrongdoing.

Since all of the contributors' names have been published within the last month . . .

So, it seems clear that we must refuse to deal with the terrorists.

Replace the entire list of class officers. *Then* we can expect to see immediate results.

As a result of his opponent's poor campaigning, the vice-president showed an early lead in the polls.

Consequently, the employees need a longer lunch break.

Because of her exceptional grades, Traci won three scholarships.

Terri left immediately *on account of* the overwhelming embarrassment of facing the crowd of hecklers.

Many South American countries have failed to control their own logging industries. *Therefore,* it seems certain that rain forest depletion will continue for at least several more years.

The library's board of trustees has decided to spend a major part of this year's revenue on remodeling the reference room. *Because of this,* the library has been forced to close its doors on Saturdays.

A Whole Essay

The following essay was written to convince readers that city and state governments must not be allowed to dispose of garbage in the ocean. Read the essay and answer the questions that follow it.

Clint Kabele
Composition II
Ms. Kelly
October 12, 19_____

Our Polluted Oceans

Ocean dumping. That term shocks most people, yet the problem is real, and it is happening today. Maybe it wouldn't sound so bad if everyone defined it the way Ed Koch, the former mayor of New York City, put it: "Finding refuge for certain wastes and by-products in an inexpensive and relatively easy way by depositing them offshore." What he is really saying is that New York City and other large metropolitan areas are dumping wastes in the ocean, one of the most beautiful and fascinating habitats on this earth. If dumping wastes in the ocean is not one of the most inhumane things to do, it is one of the most insensitive. Ocean dumping must be outlawed.

Although small amounts of waste will probably do little harm, large amounts destroy ocean life by spreading diseases and depleting the water of its oxygen supply. The fish and other inhabitants of the ocean must live in waters infested with medical debris, chemicals such as copper, lead, arsenic, zinc, and cadmium, loads of wet sludge released underwater in great black clouds, and balls of sewage two inches thick. Sounds disgusting, doesn't it?

Don't stop reading now because we're just getting to the results. East Coast fishermen have been hauling in fish with ugly red lesions on their bellies and fins that are rotting away. At least 750 dolphins have mysteriously washed up on the coast of Maine in the past eighteen months, their snouts, flippers, and tails pocked with blisters and huge patches of skin missing. In North Carolina people have been hauling up lobsters and crabs with gaping holes in their shells. As many as 2,000,000 sea birds and 100,000 marine animals die each year when they become entangled in fish line or nonbiodegradable plastic.

Sea turtles choke to death on plastic bags they mistake for jellyfish. Sea lions are ensnared when they playfully poke their noses into plastic nets and rings. Some, unable to open their jaws, simply starve to death.

A secondary result is that ocean dumping is posing a serious threat to the whole seafood industry. In the diet-and-wellness-conscious eighties, fish was widely touted as a healthful food. But it has been proven that fish and shellfish that have absorbed toxins can indirectly pass the contaminants on to humans. The incidence of illnesses from eating contaminated fish is rising around the United States. Commercial fishing is a $3.1 billion industry, and it is increasingly threatened. Smaller and smaller catches mean higher prices. This, combined with the fear of contaminated seafood, is causing more people to think twice before going out to get seafood. New York state officials have warned women of childbearing age and children under fifteen against consuming more than one-half pound of bluefish a week; they should never eat striped bass caught off Long Island.

Finally, garbage dumping pollutes coastal waters and beaches, affecting vacationers, home owners, and resort operators. Many of New York's public beaches have been closed. On the sands of the Texas Gulf Coast one day last September, volunteers collected 307 tons of litter, two-thirds of which was plastic, including 31,733 bags, 30,295 bottles, and 15,631 six-pack yokes. Pollution makes the water about as safe to swim in as an unflushed toilet.

Congress should seriously consider action to stop ocean dumping. We know that pollutants can be dispersed over hundreds of square miles by tides, currents, wave action, huge underwater columns of swirling water called rings, and deep ocean storms caused by earthquakes and volcanos. We must do something about the problem before the effect is irreversible. In dollars, pollution costs billions; the cost in the quality of life is incalculable.

DISCUSS

1. What is the thesis of Clint's essay?
2. List the subpoints that support the thesis.
3. What is the specific function of those subpoints? Does Clint show the causes or the effects of ocean dumping? What is his ultimate purpose in the essay?
4. Look at his first subpoint. In what ways is it well developed? How could it be improved?
5. Clint devotes three paragraphs to his first subpoint. Why do you think he divided it that way instead of making one long paragraph? What are the advantages of his choice? The disadvantages?

ACT
!!

Your school's homecoming football game is scheduled for the end of next week. Student committees have been organized and each is busy with its responsibilities. On the weekend before homecoming, students will decorate the halls, competing for trophies for "most original idea," "best show of school spirit," and "best use of homecoming theme." Homecoming queen candidates will be presented at an all-school assembly Monday morning, students will vote during the week, and the queen will be announced at another assembly on Thursday. On Friday, classes will be dismissed at 1:00 so everyone can either take part in or watch the big parade at 2:00. The game is scheduled for Friday night, and a semiformal dance will be held Saturday night from 9:00 until 12:30.

Your chemistry teacher, Mr. Arquit, is nearing the end of an important unit this week, but it's been tough going. There are twenty-three students in the class, and several of them are gone every day—not the same students each time, but always enough to make keeping the class together difficult. One day the parade committee met, the next day it was the assembly committee, and on the third day four students were late for class because the marching band's special practice ran late. That's when Mr. Arquit blew up.

"This homecoming situation has gotten out of hand. It's not even homecoming week yet, and several of you are so far behind, you can't possibly be ready for the test Friday."

When one student suggested that the test could have been timed to come either before homecoming activities or during the week following the homecoming game, Mr. Arquit was florid.

"It's not always possible to schedule your academic responsibilities so that they don't interfere with extracurricular events. Nor is it fair to think teachers should be the only ones to adjust. If I were to follow your suggestion, we would have had a test last Friday, and then gone into a holding pattern for two weeks while you prepare for homecoming.

"Next week the queen candidate assembly will cut our class in half. Tuesday and Wednesday a lot of you will be gone for more committee meetings and special band practices. Thursday we'll have another short class following the announcement of the queen, and Friday this whole place will shut down at 1:00 for the parade. I don't know how we can justify crippling classes this week and wrecking them completely next week. Half the teachers in the building are frustrated and angry. What we should do is just cancel homecoming next year. I've seriously considered making that suggestion at the next Principal's Advisory Committee meeting. At the very least, we need to get our priorities straight."

For your essay assignment, choose one of the following attitudes as your purpose.

1. You can see that Mr. Arquit is serious, and, even though you don't agree, he does mean well. He is honestly concerned about homecoming's effect on the learning process. He also has a reputation that will make any recommendation from him be taken seriously.

Write a letter to the Principal's Advisory Committee showing why homecoming activities are worth any disruption they may bring about. Use cause-effect reasoning to show what students gain from planning and carrying out all the related activities. Try to show that, with the right attitude, the whole thing can be a positive part of the students' education.

2. You enjoy homecoming, but you have to agree with Mr. Arquit at least to some extent. Write a letter to the Principal's Advisory Committee showing why the disruptions caused by homecoming activities are so great that some changes are needed. Use cause-effect reasoning to show that the purpose of the school is being defeated during this period.

6

Definition

Sometimes discussions turn into quarrels, not so much because of honest differences of opinion, but because the participants are vague about the meanings of the terms they use. The following scene shows how much heat and little light can be generated when people use the same terms for different meanings.

Karla went home from school still steaming from the argument in English class. Actually, the problem had started at the Fall Sports Recognition Assembly, which was held just before English class. By the time class began, several students were really wound up, and Mr. Murphy had allowed them to talk it out.

The problem began when the volleyball team was ignored at the assembly. The student council president called the football team forward, the cross-country team was recognized, and the swim team was also honored. But the volleyball team was ignored.

As soon as they got to class, Jenny said "It's just not fair. The same thing happens every year. Football gets all the attention. Nobody cares about any other sports at this school."

Jack interrupted her. "Come on, Jenny. The cross-country team got the same amount of time as any other group today. The volleyball team just didn't have a successful season. That's all."

"No, that's not the point," said Jenny. "For years the football types have gotten all the attention, and now that girls have some real sports to take part in, nobody pays any attention."

Kay followed her lead. "That's right. When our mothers were in school, the only thing they could do was be cheerleaders for the boys. There was nothing wrong with that, but it wasn't enough. Now that we can do more things, we still don't get the fan support or the money that's necessary. Nobody takes us seriously."

"Yeah, but girls would get more attention if they played real sports," claimed Keith. "Who wants to watch a bunch of girls knock a ball back and forth, anyway? I've got as much school spirit as anybody, but volleyball is boring. Besides, it doesn't take that much athletic ability. The only sport that makes a real athlete is football."

Karla fixed him with a look of complete disgust and wasn't going to dignify Keith's comment with an answer. But Jenny wasn't about to let him get away with it. "Keith, you'll never change. You think that if a sport doesn't involve violence, it can't be worth doing. Athletes aren't just the brawny types. And sports aren't just a matter of smashing the other team until they can't get up. If you went to a volleyball game, you'd know better."

Edwardo broke in. "Kay, you're half right. Maybe the football team gets most of the attention, but it's not a matter of the boys against the girls. Sure, the cross-country team got recognition today, but they had to go to the state finals to be noticed. I'm on the golf team, and we've never even been mentioned around here. I'll bet most of you didn't know the school had a golf team."

"Golf isn't a sport," said Keith. "Not the way I mean the word, anyway. Nothing personal, but if you're going to call it a sport, it has to involve some good, hard work. And be difficult. You can play a round of golf and never break a sweat."

"That's not what makes a sport," answered Edwardo.

Troy added, "Keith's right. It has to be more physical. Look at basketball. You have to be in good physical condition for that. It's not as violent as football, but it calls for some real physical and mental skills. And you have to be in good shape."

Kay spoke up again. "What's the point here? Are we talking about girls not getting the same support as boys, or are we saying some sports don't get the same fan support as others? Or are we just saying people aren't fair when they spread their school spirit around? Every one of you is talking about something different."

When nobody answered, Kay went on. "I think it's a matter of people's attitudes about the traditional 'major' sports. For years everybody, students and parents, went to basketball and football games. Boys' basketball, by the way. Those have always been popular. Now, even though schools sponsor other sports, everybody still thinks the only way to show school spirit is to scream your head off at a football game."

"Come on," said Keith. "Next you'll want us to be out cheering for the chess team."

"Actually, that doesn't sound totally ridiculous to the chess players," said Terri. "I belong to the Bicycle Touring Club, and this school certainly does nothing for us."

At this point Mr. Murphy interrupted. "Maybe we should see if there is something we can agree on here. You all seem to go along with the idea that different activities call for different talents. Some call for more practice, some more agility, and some more mental effort.

"It seems to me the real issue is what we mean when we use the term *sport*. And, for that matter, maybe we need to clarify what we mean by an *athlete*."

"And *fair*," added Keith. "What do these people want when they say something's *unfair*? Do we have to go to every activity in the school just to be fair?"

"Good question," said Mr. Murphy. "My guess is that all of you, if you thought about it for awhile, could explain what you have in mind when you talk about *sports*, and *fair*, too, for that matter. What do we, as Keith said, want when we say treatment should be fair? Would it have been enough if the volleyball team had been given a cheer this morning? Is that really all you want? Until we settle what those terms mean, this whole argument is going nowhere."

Jenny agreed. "Well, it seems obvious to me that we've got about three or four meanings of *sport* here. Maybe Keith and I could agree some day on what is fair, but we'll never get together on what is or isn't a sport."

"How about if we aim for understanding each other first and worry about agreement later," said Mr. Murphy. "At least understanding sounds like a good place to start."

Abstract and Concrete Language

Whenever you get into serious discussion about a topic that is at all involved, you are almost certain to have a second, unnoticed, level of disagreement. You are probably quite aware of the first level of disagreement. You say that *Gone With the Wind* is an unforgettable movie. Your friend doesn't agree. That much is obvious.

What is not so obvious is what either of you means when you call a movie *unforgettable*. What are your standards? One of the most frequent causes of disagreement is people's failure to clarify terms that may have several interpretations. Until the two of you can base your discussion of what is or is not an *unforgettable* movie on the same criteria, you will never understand each other. It is entirely possible that if you both defined your terms, you might find that you and your friend are not all that far from agreement.

Some words, such as *house, table, Aunt Kate,* or *run,* are concrete. They refer to objects, living things, or activities that you can see, feel, hear, or otherwise know through your senses. They are image-producing words.

Terms like *respect, love, patriotism,* and *exploitation,* on the other hand, refer to concepts that cannot be known directly through the senses. You can experience respect, love, patriotism, and exploitation through your mind, but they cannot be touched, tasted, seen, or heard. These non-image producing words are abstractions.

Since there is nothing concrete to which they can directly refer, abstractions almost always suggest different meanings to different people. If you use words like *love, tolerance,* and *freedom* in writing, without defining what you mean, you and your reader can easily be thinking about two entirely different ideas.

For instance, *sport,* to Keith, apparently means a strenuous physical activity that involves some sort of mock combat. It is a physical struggle, pitting one group of people against another. To Karla, *sports* means a physical contest between two teams, but actual body contact has nothing to do with it. To Edwardo, *sports* involves competition, probably personal but not necessarily physical, and individual skill and performance are important factors.

Each student has a different reaction to the word *sport,* and their reactions to the concept of what is *fair* or *unfair* are so far apart that you can only hope they will someday begin to understand each other. For the moment, agreement seems out of the question. But they can make a start toward understanding each other when every one of them can define exactly what he or she means by the terms *sport* and *fair.*

It would be less confusing if you could always write and speak in concrete terms, but quite often people need to use abstract language if they are going to discuss anything more important than some rock star's latest divorce. When you talk about your values and beliefs, you cannot rely on concrete language alone. There is no way to discuss the ideas of *trust, betrayal,* or *love* without using abstract terms. The danger lies in using the terms carelessly and in not clarifying what you mean. Abstract words create the illusion that a subject is simple when it may not be. For instance, saying "She is a *very religious* person" gives the impression that we have a reasonably complete picture of that person's character. Not true. She may attend church every Sunday, but do nothing else. It all depends on what you mean by very religious.

SUMMARY

Concrete words stand for real things that can be detected by the senses. You can see, hear, smell, taste, or touch what the concrete word refers to. Abstract words describe ideas, qualities, and attitudes. They refer to concepts you know through your mind, but not your senses. They are non-image producing words. The meanings of abstract words can be ambiguous and will vary from one person to another.

DISCUSS

1. How can abstract words cause a second level of disagreement in a discussion? Explain one example of your own.
2. How can abstract words encourage the idea that a subject is very simple when it is not? Explain one example of your own.

ACT

1. Reread the story about Karla's dispute with her classmates. List ten abstract words or phrases in the story. The most obvious examples are *sports* and *fair,* but words like *recognized* are also abstract.
2. Pick three of the words you listed above and explain what characteristics of abstract language each word has. Then explain two ways each could be interpreted.

FOR YOUR JOURNAL

In *Gulliver's Travels,* Jonathan Swift's hero visits the Grand Academy of Lagado. There, in the school of languages, professors are at work on "a scheme for entirely abolishing all words whatsoever." They reasoned that "since words are only names for *things,* it would be more convenient to carry about them such things as were necessary to express the particular business they are to discuss on." Gulliver says that he has often seen these "sages almost sinking under the weight of their packs, like pedlars . . . who, when they meet in the streets, would lay down their loads, open their sacks, and hold conversation for an hour."

In your journal, write down your thoughts on this scheme. Are words really "only names for things"? Would the scheme allow for the expression of abstract ideas? If not, would this be good or bad? Why? Would the scheme make it possible for people to avoid misunderstanding each other?

You might use this incident from *Gulliver's Travels* as the basis for a brief essay on the relation between words and things. Like Swift, you might take a humorous approach.

Scale of Abstraction

One final word about abstract and concrete language. Words do not exist in neat little boxes labeled *concrete* and *abstract.* Their relationship bears more resemblance to a musical scale, with a range all the way from extreme concreteness to extreme abstraction. Levels of abstraction are invariably a matter of degree, and the label you attach to a word usually exists somewhere between the two extremes. For instance, *transportation* and *my 1991 Grand Am* are far apart on the scale of abstraction, with *my 1991 Grand Am* being the most concrete and *transportation* being the most abstract. Between them, you can have several levels of concreteness and abstraction.

transportation
> *vehicle*
>> *automobile*
>>> *American auto*
>>>> *Pontiac*
>>>>> *my 1991 Grand Am*

As your eyes descend from *transportation* to *vehicle* to *automobile,* and eventually land on one car, each step is more and more easy for you to picture. Any scale of abstraction will illustrate the same relationship.

vacation
      travel
            flight
                 airline
                        TWA
                             Flight 310

human rights
      constitutional rights
            free speech
                 freedom of press
                       editorial page
                           John's column

SUMMARY

Language is neither wholly abstract nor wholly concrete. How a word is classified is a matter of degree, and there are many degrees or levels of concreteness and abstraction.

DISCUSS

1. Why is it misleading to think of words as being exclusively abstract or exclusively concrete?
2. Why is the musical scale an appropriate way to show the relative abstraction or concreteness of a set of words?

ACT

Name four abstract words that you have heard or seen recently. Put each on a scale of abstraction by naming one related word that is more concrete and one related word that is more abstract.

Types of Definition

During a discussion, it's not unusual for one person to challenge another by demanding "Define your terms. What exactly do you mean by *racist*?"

The problem caused by terms having more than one meaning is not restricted to discussion, of course. It crops up all the time in writing. The difference is that a reader can't ask, "Just what do you mean by *racist*?" You, the writer, have to foresee the reader's unspoken question and be ready to answer it.

When faced with the need to define your terms, you have a choice of methods. If the word is fairly uncomplicated, you can use the dictionary approach. If the word and your definition are complicated, you'll want to use an extended definition.

Dictionary Definition

A dictionary definition typically defines a word by first putting it in a general class and then differentiating it from others in the class. For instance, *widow* is first classified as "a woman" and then differentiated from other women by saying that she is one "whose husband is dead." Similarly, *slave* is placed in the classification "human being" and then differentiated by adding "who is owned by another." Here are some more dictionary definitions.

Term	*Classification*	*Differentiation*
1. seamstress	woman	whose occupation is sewing
2. optician	person	who makes or sells eyeglasses
3. misgiving	feeling	of fear or doubt
4. budget	plan	adjusting expenses to income
5. Buenos Aires	capital	of Argentina
6. Brooklyn	borough	of New York City

Depending on the word being defined, the differentiation may be simple or involved.

7. paranoia	mental condition	characterized by delusions of grandeur or persecution
8. lottery	game of chance	in which people buy numbered tickets for prizes, and winners are chosen through a drawing

A second kind of dictionary definition, the synonym, is often used. *Davenport* means *couch*, and *tablet* means *pill*. The synonym is useful when used carefully, but too often, if the word being defined is unfamiliar, so is the synonym. *Vorticity* means *vortical motion,* and *Markoff process* means a *stochastic process*. Is that clear?

Extended Definition

In situations where you need to clarify abstract or controversial words, such as *creativity, success, patriotism,* or *sport,* the dictionary definition will probably not allow you to give enough information. To effectively define such words, you need to expand the dictionary definition, anywhere from a paragraph to an entire book.

Often, the writer of an extended definition wants to persuade as well as define. When philosopher and educator Mortimer Adler wrote *How to Read a Book*, he did more than give advice on reading. He wrote a book-length definition of the word *read*, and in the process promoted his ideas about the process of learning.

If Terri wrote a letter to Ms. Trampel, the activities coordinator of her high school, and in that letter she presented her interpretation of the term *sport*, you could assume that she was doing so with the intention of convincing Ms. Trampel that the Bicycle Touring Club should be included in that definition. Her purpose would be to see that the club received the same financial and legal recognition as any other athletic group in the school.

The extended definition offers you the chance to not only explain what you mean by a word but present your reader with reasons why he or she should feel compelled to accept your definition as correct. In the sense that it encourages people to change their attitudes, an extended definition can become almost a moral argument.

Since the extended definition is both the most involved and the most useful form of definition, the remainder of this chapter will concentrate on writing the extended definition.

SUMMARY

The definitions you are most likely to use are the dictionary definition and the extended definition. Dictionary definitions work well for concrete words and for uncomplicated concepts. However, if you want to be clear about the interpretation of an important word, an extended definition will be necessary.

DISCUSS

1. Under what circumstances would you expect a dictionary definition to be adequate? What kind of word could be explained this way? Give one example, and tell why the dictionary definition would be complete enough.

2. Under what circumstances might an extended definition become necessary? What kind of word might call for an extended definition? Give one example, and tell why the extended definition is necessary.

ACT

Without using a dictionary, make up a concise, one-sentence definition for these words. Be sure to define the word by first putting it in a general class and then differentiating it from others in the class.

house	senator
window	chair
brick	table

FOR YOUR JOURNAL

You and your friends have probably been referred to collectively by several names: *youth, teenagers, kids, young adults,* or *youngsters.* What is the difference in how you interpret each of these terms? Which is the most agreeable? The least? Under what circumstances would you expect to hear each of them used? Are there other terms that are also used? What are they?

Take a page or two of your journal to explain how you feel about the names used for people your age. Do you think people sometimes have bad motives for the terms they use? Do they use one word when they want something, and another when they just don't care? Do you suppose they are uncomfortable, not knowing what you would like to be called? Have you ever been uncomfortable at not knowing what to call someone?

Methods of Extended Definition

Extended definitions don't follow just one pattern. There are many approaches. The approach you choose depends on the particular word and what you have to say about it.

Naming Characteristics

In naming the characteristics of a term, you must limit yourself to qualities that are distinctive to that term. That is, the characteristics must make your word stand out from all others like it. For instance, if you are defining *totalitarianism,* it does little good to say that it is an oppressive form of government. Many forms of government are considered oppressive in one way or another. What distinguishes a totalitarian regime are the number and kinds of controls it exerts over its subjects. You need to point out and explain that the press is run by the government, churches are state controlled, free assembly is denied, and citizens are not allowed freedom of movement.

If you are going to define your idea of *courtesy,* you will want to point out that it involves respect for others' rights, consideration of others' feelings, and sympathy for others' needs. Not everyone may agree with you, but the point is that you have listed the characteristics that you believe distinguish *courtesy* from other virtues.

Offering Examples

Giving examples is probably the most direct way to explain your meaning of a word. If you are defining a *good meal,* naming the characteristics of that meal is necessary and helpful, but showing exactly what will be on the table encourages the reader's imagination to smell and taste the food. A detailed description of a Mario's Combination Extra Cheese Pizza with pepperoni, Italian sausage, and Canadian bacon, accompanied by bread sticks and Pepsi, will give a much more accurate idea of what you have in mind than simply saying the meal must have meat, vegetables, bread, and beverage included.

If you are defining your idea of *impressive architecture,* your point will be more easily understood if you include the pyramid-shaped Transamerica Building in San Francisco or the gargoyle-covered Chrysler Building in New York.

Explaining the Purpose

"What is it supposed to do?" is a normal question to expect when you are defining a *positive attitude,* an *ideal vacation,* or a *good teacher.* In many cases the function of your term may be the most important part of the definition. The function of a *psychiatrist* is central to the meaning of the term. Defining an *indispensable tool* or *conscience* without telling what they do is virtually impossible.

There may be times when explaining the purpose of something seems of minor importance. For instance, the purpose of *brotherhood* may seem pointless and difficult to pin down, compared to the ease with which you could describe its characteristics and give an example. With some abstractions, the question of function is not even appropriate. *Conservatism, being in need,* and *good taste* are terms that will never bring the idea of function to mind. In that case, concentrate on other, more appropriate methods of definition.

Comparing and Contrasting

A word can be made clear and less likely to confuse by showing how it is similar to or different from related words. A definition of *love* might be clearer if you can show how it is different from *infatuation.* A paper on *atheism* might be better if you compared the idea to *agnosticism. Good sportsmanship* will be clearer if you can also show what you mean by *bad sportsmanship,* and one of the best ways to define *masculine* might be to contrast it with *feminine.*

Another form of comparison and contrast is negation. It is often helpful to include a reference to what your abstraction is not. "By small-scale business, I do not mean one of those nationally franchised fast-food shops that sells pizza by the slice in a mall, or a drive-through Chinese food franchise that costs $500,000 in start-up money. Employing only three people does not make them small-scale. They cost entirely too much for the average person's investment."

If you use negation as a part of your definition, be sure to point out why the alternative example is not what you have in mind. Show, for example, how the fast-food Chinese drive-through does not match the characteristics you have established. In this case it costs too much.

Using Analogy

An analogy compares things that are basically different by discussing one of them in terms of the other. It is a comparison of a common quality found in dissimilar things.

You may, for example, find it useful to describe a *corporation* in terms of a *family,* or *creativity* in terms of *fireworks.* Your idea of *ineffective education* might be made clearer if you compare it to a *soft drink machine* pumping out identical cans of soda.

You may occasionally find analogies useful. The danger is that readers are so used to analogies in sportswriting that all but the most original ones sound like cliches. Use them at your own risk. Certainly, you would never base a whole definition on an analogy.

Combining Approaches

You may have noticed that some of the methods of definition overlap. It is very possible that your comparison and contrast could sound a lot like examples. This should not cause you any problems. Remember that the purpose is to explain your idea to the reader, not to have a neat label you can attach to each method of explanation. When you write an extended definition essay, you most likely will use a combination of several of the methods shown here. You might write the essay without even thinking about the methods you are using. Knowledge of the different methods is most useful when you are having trouble thinking of how to explain yourself, and you need some ideas. In that situation, think of how you could apply each method to your situation.

For instance, if you are still trying to define what you mean by *great architecture,* you might use the methods in this way.

-Characteristics
imaginative
exciting
appropriate for the location
attractive

-Examples
West Wacker Building, Chicago

Pennzoil Place, Houston
Texas Commerce Tower, Dallas

-Purpose

Great architecture is an artistic outlet. Quote Philip Johnson, architect of Pennzoil Place: "A skyscraper is an emotional term; it talks about ambition."

-Compare and Contrast

"The John Hancock Center is an exciting example of modern architecture, but the Brunswick Building lacks imagination and excitement."

-Analogy

Quote architect Louis Sullivan comparing great architecture to a living thing with human pride: "Every inch a proud and soaring thing, rising in sheer exultation."

Architect Henry Cobb said, "Geometry pursued with rigor." Expand on the analogies.

No one of these methods adequately defines great architecture, but in combination, they communicate one person's picture of what the term means.

SUMMARY

You can develop an extended definition essay by (1) naming characteristics, (2) giving examples, (3) explaining purpose, (4) comparing and contrasting, or (5) giving analogies. In practice most people use a combination of two or more of these methods. The best approach is to use the methods as sources of ideas when you are at the brainstorming stage of developing your definition.

DISCUSS

1. When naming characteristics, why is it crucial that you concentrate on qualities that are distinctive to the term you are defining?
2. Name three abstract terms in which the function of the word being defined should be included in its definition. Why is it important in each?
3. A comparison can sometimes sound like an example, and an analogy is always some form of comparison. To what degree is it important if methods of definition begin to overlap? Why?

ACT

For each term listed below, pick one of the methods of definition and explain how that method could be used to explain your interpretation of the word. Be sure to use each of the methods at least once.

grammar	peace
competition	moral
optimist	pessimism
family	style
reckless driving	classy

Writing a Definition Essay

Writing a definition essay is appropriate when you are using a key term that is abstract or controversial, or when your interpretation of that term is different from the accepted definition.

Checklist for Writers

1. Your thesis should be built on the interpretation you intend to give your key term. For instance, if *athlete* is your key term and you believe that an athlete is someone whose skill, strength, and stamina can be applied successfully to several sports, not just one, your thesis should reflect that belief.

2. Try to use several methods to develop your definition. Brainstorm characteristics possessed by athletes, create a list of people you could compare and contrast, pick out examples of athletes you admire, and distinguish between your meaning of *athlete* and any other meanings that some people might be inclined to include. "Mario Andretti may be a very good race-car driver, but he is no athlete."

3. It is unlikely that one method alone will clarify the term sufficiently. It is just as unlikely that you will use all of the methods for one definition. For instance, function may not be appropriate for *athlete*. Use those methods that are most effective, and don't try to set records for

number of methods used. The best approach: try them all and use those that work the best.

4. Plan to arrange your supporting explanations in an order of importance. There is no ironclad rule to guide you here. Just be certain that you have an introduction that ends with your thesis statement. Follow that with several paragraphs that clarify your interpretation of the word. Finish with one of the standard methods of conclusion.

SUMMARY

In definition, as with any writing assignment, it helps to have a set procedure to follow. Begin by building your thesis on the interpretation you give the word. Then, try to apply all the methods of definition, but use only those that work the best. Finally, plan to arrange your explanations in an order of importance. If you follow these steps, you can concentrate on content instead of worrying about form.

DISCUSS

Read the following essay and be prepared to discuss the questions that follow it.

Matt Groe
Composition II
November 1, 19_____

The American Dream

America is supposed to be the home of the fulfilled dream. It is the place where anyone can find an interesting job, make a decent living, and be happy. But is it? The truth is that many people barely get by. Anyone who is incapable of living a happy and fulfilled life in our society is truly needy.

The most obviously needy people are the homeless. They need food, clothing, and shelter. Many of them live day-to-day, making money by begging, prostitution, or robbery, while others eat what they can find in the garbage. They sleep in dumpsters, on benches, and on the ground, no matter what the weather is like. They have no family. Nobody cares for them. They are truly needy. On the other hand, while food, clothing, and shelter are necessary for a full life, it's possible that a person could have these things and still be truly needy.

Anyone who does not have a good education is usually doomed to a life of hard physical work, little pay, and little time for pleasure. To get a decent job that will pay much more than minimum wage in today's world, you need at least a high school diploma, and every day it is getting more and more difficult to find a good job that doesn't require a college education. Now, more than ever, education is becoming a necessity. People who lack it usually end up in low-income jobs, such as food service or janitorial work, that offer little chance of promotion.

People in these jobs barely make enough to support themselves, let alone a family. To provide for a family, both parents have to work all the hours they can get. Despite their efforts, they often end up living in poor housing and getting by with too little food, clothing, and time together. Their children could never afford college and often drop out of high school to help support the family. At the end of their lifetimes, their wrinkled faces and calloused hands tell a tale of misery.

Another thing that can cause misery is continuing poor health. People in poor health who can't afford medical treatments and operations are needy. For example, some people who have extreme cases of arthritis go through torture every day because they can't afford drugs and treatments that would ease their pain and let them live normal lives. Also, some people have diseases, like cancer or leukemia, that are very difficult to cure. Some of them can't afford the treatments and operations that could prolong their lives by months or years.

Even for families that can afford the treatments and operations, sometimes it takes all of their money, and they are left with little to live on. I've read about families that need food and clothing because all the parents' income goes to pay for medicine needed to keep their children alive. They shouldn't have to take on that burden alone.

However, money isn't all that matters. Even people who have money can have health problems that ruin their lives and make them truly needy. For instance, many people need organ transplants and can't find suitable donors. There are also people who suffer from incurable diseases such as Acquired Immune Deficiency Syndrome or muscular dystrophy. They know that they are doomed to a short, painful life. Under these conditions no one could live a happy and enriched life.

Furthermore, everyone has needs beyond the physical, and to deny these needs is cruel and inhumane. People who lack love, attention, appreciation, and companionship will have terrible lives filled with self-torment. Many times these problems lead to insanity or suicide. They also lead some to drug addiction, alcoholism, or eating disorders such as anorexia. Just a little love or companionship could turn these people into happy and productive workers, but if they go unhelped, they will never get anywhere in life.

Our society has a responsibility to help those who cannot by their own power live happy lives filled with opportunities to enrich themselves. If we do this, we will be making the American dream a reality.

1. What is the thesis for this definition essay? How well is it stated?
2. List the supporting points for the thesis. What major characteristics of the truly needy does Matt intend to develop?
3. Analyze any two body paragraphs. If they are well developed, what development do you see? If they are not well developed, explain what additional development should take place.
4. How concrete is Matt in giving us a picture of truly needy people?
5. How good is the introduction? Explain.
6. How good is the conclusion? Explain.

ACT !!

Write a carefully structured essay of 500 to 700 words in which you develop and explain your own views about an abstraction that is important to you.

For instance, if you choose a word like *freedom,* be sure to discuss the kinds of freedoms you think a person should or shouldn't have, and how far those freedoms should go. Use plenty of examples to show what kinds of freedoms you have in mind. Since your audience is mainly people in your own community, be sure to use examples that will be familiar and convincing to them.

Remember, part of your purpose is to convince your readers that they should share your opinion, so be sure to plan the essay with that in mind.

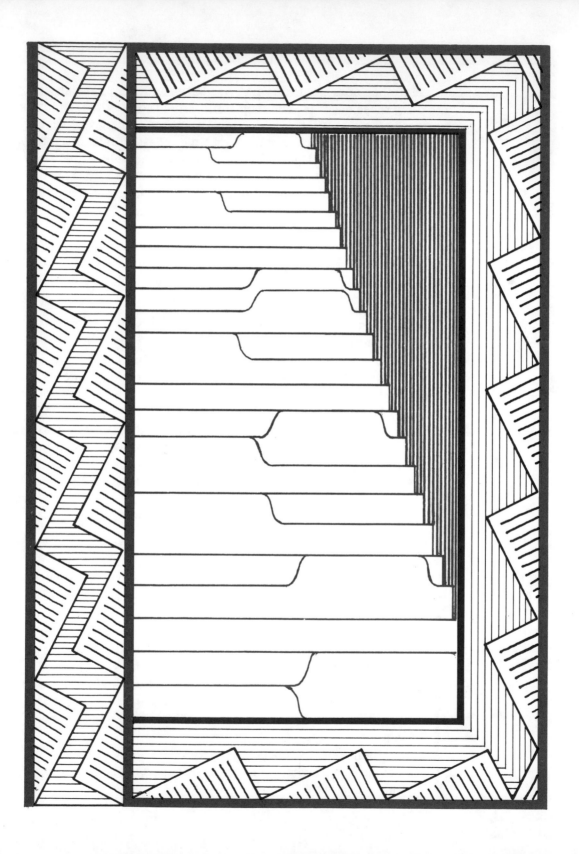

7

The Classification Essay

The human mind is more complex than most people ever consider. It is a storehouse of memories and the source of a constant stream of original, unique thought. Some people can multiply complex figures in their head. Others learn several languages. Even those who think mastering one language is difficult have thousands of words stored away in their mind. Besides the words, they know hundreds of usage rules and apply them without ever having to consciously think about them.

Usage rules may actually be among the simpler things you store in your mind. You also have stored away a map of the United States. You probably could label each of the states with its name and capital city. As a matter of fact, you probably have stored away hundreds of maps of various sizes and complexities. You have a very detailed map of your own neighborhood, and a slightly less detailed map of your hometown, and you could name dozens of cities and towns in your state. Certainly, you have a very good idea of where these places are in relation to your own location.

You can even travel mentally outside of the United States and, chances are, you can name and accurately locate dozens of foreign countries without straining. You have a mental picture of what natives of the various countries look like, and you could probably supply a lot of information about each country you remember.

Human beings carry massive amounts of information around with them, ready for instant use. Most people make complex calculations every time they go to a shopping mall. If you are trying to decide whether to buy a leather jacket that's on sale, your mind has to sort and balance several categories of information: cost, quality, and appearance. Is this a reasonable price? How does it compare with the price at competing stores? Is the quality adequate? Will the store stand behind the product? Does the jacket look good on you? Will the style last? Will the price be even better next week? Is there something else you would rather spend your money on? Will it look good with your other clothes?

Luckily, you probably don't consciously think about those questions every time you buy something. You would drive yourself crazy. But your brain is quietly doing its job—sorting, categorizing, classifying. And when you need to make a decision, chances are your brain can process all that information and supply you with the correct answer.

It's doubtful that anyone fully understands how that three-pound mass of tissue controls ten billion nerve cells and efficiently handles all your mental functions. Today, brain-research scientists are learning more and more about the parts and individual functions of the brain, but it will undoubtedly be a long time before scientists have a complete picture of how it handles so much information. There is one fact, however, of which you can be sure. Your mind is constantly classifying the information it receives.

The Mind Needs Order

The human mind needs a filing system—that much is certain. It can learn more, and function better and faster when knowledge is organized. The concept of systematically organizing knowledge is so common to human experience that it is almost automatic. When you walk into a library, you expect to be able to locate a book quickly and easily according to a commonly accepted system of classification. The Dewey decimal classification system has been used since the late 1800s in libraries all over the world. According to this system, all knowledge is divided into ten categories. The numbers 000 to 099 include encyclopedias, newspapers, and other general collections of information. Philosophy and psychology are numbered from 100 to 199, books dealing with religion are classified from 200 to 299, and so on to 900 to 999, which includes geography and history.

Each of those ten classifications is broken into ten subclasses, each of which contains ten more subclasses, which are further divided by adding decimal places. In every library using the Dewey system you can be certain that books numbered 810 to 819 will deal with American literature, and, more specifically, you can be assured that a book numbered 813.46 will be about the American writer Henry James. In the same way, any book numbered 808 will be about creative writing. Since each of these classifications has been very specifically defined, every librarian in the world has a system for filing books that will assure uniformity with all other libraries using the same system.

People use classification systems in all areas of human knowledge. Science organizes living things by the structures of their bodies. The physical elements are listed according to another system called the periodic table. Your school even classifies areas of knowledge into departments, and more specific groups of information are broken into individual courses. Those courses are separated still further into units of study.

When you divide large bodies of knowledge into logical parts, you enable your mind to make sense of what you already know by seeing relationships between the pieces of information. Without classification, systematic thought would be impossible.

SUMMARY

Classification is a method of grasping a complex subject. It is a way of breaking something down into its parts and examining them one at a time. Classification also creates order and meaning out of experience. In fact, when you classify, you discover new knowledge as you observe relationships between the pieces of information that you have. The human mind appreciates order.

DISCUSS

1. Why is classification so necessary when dealing with everyday experiences?
2. How does classification help people deal with large amounts of information?

ACT

1. In as many ways as possible, classify the courses you are taking. You might arrange them first by type—social studies, science, language arts. Then you might arrange them by difficulty. Use at least three classes in each system, and place each of your courses in one of the groups. You could use levels of interest, purpose, or even kinds of classroom activities used by the teacher.

2. Classify yourself in as many ways as possible. Be sure to include political, religious, social, economic, and physical characteristics. When you have finished listing the classifications you fit into, do the same for a friend who possesses different characteristics.

FOR YOUR JOURNAL

People are often judged by the classifications they fit into, and those judgments are often resented, especially when they seem arbitrary.

In the Act section above, you classified yourself in several ways. You were born into some of those classifications, and many others probably won't change. You arrived on this earth either male or female; nobody consulted you about the matter. You are right-handed, left-handed, or ambidextrous; that probably won't change. Classifications like these seem predetermined.

Some classifications, however, are a result of deliberate choices and they can often be altered. In your journal write down your feelings about the degree to which people are responsible for their own classifications. How much choice does the average person have? Mention some examples of people who have no choice about how they are labeled. Name some instances in which people have overcome the labels others gave them. Are there some situations in which a particular classification may give a person unfair advantage over others?

Classification in Your Writing

Classification has three major purposes in your writing. First, you use classification as one of the steps in preparing to write. You spend a few minutes thinking about your topic, and you list all of the related facts or ideas you can think of to support your thesis statement. You increase your own understanding of the subject by examining all aspects of it carefully. You may think of new facts, or remember additional ones that would not have come to you without going through the process of breaking your topic into its parts.

Second, soon after brainstorming ideas for possible use in an essay, you try to cluster them into the most effective natural groups. You look for natural categories, for ideas that logically belong together. You arrange these ideas so you can see what methods of organization come to mind. These first two purposes are not much different from the steps Melvil Dewey must have gone through when he devised his library classification plan. He listed all the parts to be included in the whole, and then he grouped them into what seemed like natural categories.

The third purpose is the one on which you will concentrate in this chapter—the meanings of the classifications themselves. The question of whether someone or something belongs in a particular category may be of interest to your readers. For instance, if you divide drivers into four classes—talented novices, seasoned experts, overconfident veterans, and old-timers—it would be interesting to hear exactly what you mean by each of those terms. It might also be interesting to read why you classified one of your friends as an overconfident veteran. Used in this sense, classification becomes a method of analyzing and explaining a subject.

By the same token, if you decide to analyze the topic of abusers of legal drugs, you might want to classify these drugs as over-the-counter remedies, alcoholic beverages, and tobacco products. It would be interesting to see what you think is an unacceptable use of pain relievers, cold tablets, and cough medicines, and exactly what relationship you see between these drugstore remedies and the use of alcohol and tobacco.

In this third purpose, the classification itself becomes the main interest of the essay and actually determines the content. The classification essay becomes an essay of persuasion when you explain why you see the class as you do, and why you assign a particular example to that class.

The structure of a classification essay is usually straightforward. Each major section of your paper is devoted to one of your classifications, and each of the classifications is described as specifically as possible, usually with several examples. Each group is kept separated from the others so that there is little possibility of confusion.

Classification essays on *teachers* or *store clerks* might be organized as follows. Each section represents at least one paragraph.

I. Introduction	I. Introduction
II. Unreasonable graders	II. Businesslike clerks
III. Fair graders	III. Customer-oriented clerks
IV. Pushover graders	IV. Sleepwalking clerks
V. Conclusion	V. Conclusion

SUMMARY

Classification has three purposes in writing. First, you use the principle of breaking something into its parts in order to examine what information is available about your topic. Second, you use it to cluster those ideas into natural groupings. Third, classification can become the major interest and purpose of your essay.

DISCUSS

1. Explain the three uses of classification in writing.
2. Classification is probably used to some degree in every essay you write. Under what circumstances can classification become the main interest in an essay?

ACT

Choose four of the topics below and write an outline showing how you would use the classification method to discuss those topics. If you prefer, you may use a topic of your own.

Hobbies
Advice-givers
Smokers
Love
Coaches
Attitudes toward money
Drivers
Football fans

Example: Types of excuses for late homework assignments
      I. Introduction
     II. Old standards
    III. Plausible, but suspicious
    IV. Fairy tales
     V. Tearjerkers
   VI. Conclusion

FOR YOUR JOURNAL

Some people tend to credit luck, good or bad, for a lot of what happens to them. Others think that you make your own luck.

For instance, Timothy Dowd said, "You can't hope to be lucky. You have to prepare to be lucky," and James Austin wrote a whole essay in which he classified four types of luck. Only one of them, which he called "accident," fit the definition most of us would apply to luck. The other three were all affected by the individual's actions, and sometimes, according to Austin, even personality traits. He said that curiosity, persistence, individuality, and being observant can encourage luck to strike a person.

In your journal, write about several instances of luck you have had. Try to show how your good fortune does or does not fall into distinct classifications. Do you have different types of luck? Is some of your luck a result of your own work?

A German proverb says "There is no one luckier than he who thinks himself so." Could your luck fall into this category? Are some people convinced they are lucky, or unlucky, and good or bad things happen as a result?

Preparing to Write

When you're developing ideas for a classification essay, you'll make the job a lot easier if you keep five guidelines in mind.

Use a Limited Group

Your topic must be one that is appropriate for the length of your essay. If you are going to write an essay of about 500 to 600 words, you haven't the time to cover a topic like "animals." You might be able to write about "canine personalities" though. By the same token, it would be unrealistic to try to cover "entertainment" in 500 to 600 words. Instead, "Television detectives" might work well.

Use at Least Three Classifications

In theory, there is nothing wrong with dividing a group into just two classes. But you'll find that it doesn't give you much to work with. It may even indicate that your classifications are so obvious as to be of little interest. Also, the existence of only two classes may be a sign that you are overlooking something. Classifying politicians as good or bad covers only the extremes. A third category, the vast majority in the middle, is being ignored. And, even if you chose to discuss good politicians, bad politicians, and average politicians, you could do much better with a more imaginative set of classifications. Most of the time, you can find a third, much more interesting category if you think about the subject a few minutes. A category called "inspirational leaders," for example, is a vast improvement.

Use Personal, Original Classifications

Scientists have already classified the animal kingdom, and the Social Security Administration has classified American workers. In fact, many classification systems already exist. Your essay will be more interesting if you choose an original approach, one that reflects your own view of a subject. For instance, classifying excuses for being tardy is almost certain to be more interesting than classifying mammals of the world. Classifying your friends attracts more interest than classifying world religions.

Use One Principle of Classification

Some subjects can be classified in many ways. Cars can be classified by body style, engine size, price range, color, or prestige. Any one of these classifications would provide a reasonable basis for an essay, but you must stick to just one.

If you want to classify movies, for example, you will need to decide beforehand what basis of classification you are going to use. You can classify them by topic or by production cost or by the quality of their music. But you can't use all three without creating a hopeless jumble.

For instance, a paper that groups daytime television programs into the following classes makes no sense:

a. quiz shows
b. game shows
c. award winners

   d. talk shows
   e. news shows
   f. soap operas

The "award winners" class is not one of the natural divisions of this classification system.

Use a Personal Slant

Use the thesis sentence to include your point of view. This will give your paper an extra interest. The following thesis sentences call for more than just classifying their subjects. They indicate that the writer is going to express a point of view about each.

> Drug users, whatever their type, have crippling emotional problems.
> Every single kind of daytime television program is intellectually insulting.
> People's attitudes toward Christmas show the better side of human nature.
> Balancing, no matter how, is going to make your life a lot more enjoyable.

Any of these thesis statements makes it possible for you to include a persuasive element that gives your paper more purpose than simply breaking a topic into several types. In the first thesis sentence, you are going to tell not only about the types of drug users but also about the emotional problems associated with drug use. In the second, you are going to tell about several kinds of daytime television, but you are also going to explain what you think is wrong with each.

SUMMARY

When you plan a classification essay, be sure to choose an appropriately limited topic with at least three classifications. Choose a personally meaningful topic, and restrict yourself to one principle of classification. Finally, try to express an original point of view about the subject.

DISCUSS

1. Explain why a writer should choose a topic with at least three classifications.
2. Why is it necessary to use only one principle of classification in an essay?
3. Point out the possible weaknesses in each of the following outlines for a classification essay. You may see more than one problem in an outline.

A. Careers
   I. Industry
   II. Government

B. College Students
   I. Year
   II. Sex
   III. Major
   IV. Grades

C. Drivers
   I. Women drivers
   II. Truck drivers
   III. Good drivers
   IV. Poor drivers

D. Major American Religions
   I. Catholic
   II. Jewish
   III. Protestant

E. Schools
   I. Elementary
   II. High school
   III. Parochial
   IV. College

ACT

People or things can be classified in many ways, depending on a person's point of view. For example, a mechanic might classify cars by engine design, a cab company might classify them by warranty available, and a salesperson might classify them by body style. Others could be most interested in comfort or a smooth ride.

Pick some group of people or things, and classify them according to a principle you think important. In a brief outline, show how you would arrange the classes in an essay.

Then try to look at the group from another point of view, and classify the items according to a new principle. Be sure that each principle of classification is clear. Save your outline for later use.

Developing Your Essay

The process of writing your classification essay will be easier if you keep these four principles in mind.

Make Classifications Complete

Be sure that all examples of your subject will fit into one of the classes. If you have to make up a new class to fit an unusual example of your subject, do so. But if you seem to be facing an endless string of classifications, it might be wise to rethink your subject. More than five classifications could be unwieldy, and limiting the topic a bit may eliminate problems. A paper classifying television programs could go on and on, but changing the topic to television talk shows would make the essay much easier to handle.

Explain Treatment of Characteristics

You may assume that your reasoning is obvious, but a reader familiar with the subject may not agree with your description of a classification. If you purposely leave out a characteristic that you think is not appropriate, you should explain why. Otherwise, the reader may think that you are overlooking it. For instance, if you deliberately leave out the characteristic "male" from a description of Protestant clergy, be sure to explain that you feel the likelihood of Protestant clergy being one sex or the other is immaterial. The reader may not always agree with you, but it is important that he or she understands you.

On the other hand, it is possible that you may want to include a characteristic your reader might disagree with or find confusing. Some characteristics call for explanation. For example, if you are classifying types of political demonstrations, one of your classes might be "effective demonstrations." If you think an effective demonstration must be nonviolent, it would be wise to foresee that some people will not agree with you. You must explain why nonviolence is key to an effective demonstration. If, all around you, people are acting violently, you must assume that your contention is not automatically accepted by everyone. Martin Luther King, Jr., wrote just such a classification essay in his book, *Where Do We Go from Here: Chaos or Community?*

Develop Classifications Thoroughly

Depending on your topic, one classification may need a lot more explanation than the others. Leave yourself the option of explaining each classification as much or as little as necessary.

For instance, if you are classifying the types of jobs available to teenagers, it may be fairly easy to cover the fast-food variety. Many readers will be familiar with that type of work. On the other hand, some jobs can provide training and experience that apply to long-term career interests. You may find explaining that type of job and its benefits deserves more space.

Don't abuse this option by ignoring the fact that your essay should be well balanced, but if one group is much more complicated than the others, use whatever space is necessary to emphasize or expand on that classification.

Acknowledge Complications

Classification is natural and necessary, but sometimes it is complicated. Individuals you identify as belonging to one group may have some of the characteristics of another group. Or they may shift to the other group if circumstances change. People who possess good judgment can make mistakes, and people who act foolishly most of the time can have moments of real insight. A stopped clock is dead right every twelve hours. Democrats can vote for Republicans, and Republicans can switch parties just as easily. If a subject is involved enough to deserve a 600-word essay, it may present difficulties. Acknowledge these difficulties, explain how they affect your classification system, and make your judgments as clear as possible.

SUMMARY

In writing your essay, be alert to the fact that you need classifications for every possible example of your topic. Take whatever space is necessary to explain unusual treatment of a topic, and devote an appropriate amount of space to each classification of your essay. Also, recognize the fact that some persons or things may actually shift from one class to another.

DISCUSS

1. Why is it necessary to explain your reasons for including or excluding certain characteristics in your description of a classification? Make your answer as specific as possible by including an example.
2. Under what circumstances might it be permissible to make one section of your classification essay appreciably longer than the others? Give an example.

ACT

In the last Act on page 125, you picked a group of people or things and classified them. You wrote an outline that showed how you would use that classification system in an essay. The first part of your answer might have looked like this:

> Kinds of advertising
> I. Humorous
> II. Factual
> III. Special features
> IV. Bargain offers

Then, you reclassified the same group from a second point of view, according to a different principle, and outlined how you would write another essay. The second part of your answer might have looked like this:

> Kinds of advertising
> I. Prime time
> II. Saturday morning
> III. Sports events
> IV. After-school reruns

You are going to write two paragraphs. Take one classification from each outline, and write a paragraph showing how you would explain that classification.

For instance, you might choose "Bargain offers" from the first example and write a paragraph showing the distinguishing characteristics of that class. Be sure to explain fully and include at least two examples.

A Whole Essay

The following essay shows the writer's attitude toward three unusual groups of people. Read the essay and answer the questions that follow it.

Eric Hansen
Composition II
Mr. Allen
January 17, 19____

Football Fan Frenzy

Picture a subarctic winter day. The temperature drops even more as the ice-choked winds pick up strength. The only football fans present in the stadium will be the enthusiastic ones who attend every single game. Other fans, the fair-weather type, only show up for a game on a nice day, or maybe for a really important game. Still other fans won't even go to any games at all. They'll stay comfortably at home and watch on the tube. People's attitudes toward football show some interesting varieties of human nature.

The enthusiastic, die-hard fan shows up for every game, rain or shine, summer or winter. You see these people on television covered in layers of clothes, sipping hot coffee. Or, if rain looks possible, they arrive dressed in huge all-weather ponchos and carrying oversized umbrellas. On hot days, you'll probably find these fans half naked and swilling gallons of cold soda. Every day will find them wearing team colors. They never miss a game and always support their team. Half their incomes go to buying season tickets and all kinds of football paraphernalia. They'll be at a game even if their team doesn't stand a chance. Even if their team falls short of a winning season, they'll be there to the very last. During the winning seasons, they'll be there, mocking the fair-weather fan for just now deciding to show up and support a winner.

Unlike die-hard fans, fair-weather fans don't quite possess the determination to attend every single game. Usually they appear at championships, playoffs, or other important games. These are the fans you usually see leaving early when one team has the game wrapped up. Why should they stay? Who wants to watch the winning team's replacement players? Fair-weather fans dress to look and be looked at. They hardly ever ruin their image by wearing team colors or by dressing for the weather. So, if the weather becomes too hot, too wet, or too cold, these fans will be gone with the wind. Fair-weather fans are along only for the fun, and most of them couldn't care less about the results of the game. They're there to socialize. When their team starts losing, the fair-weather fans go elsewhere. These are the people you don't see on a bad day.

Contrasting with both die-hard fans and fair-weather fans are the couch-potato fans. Couch potatoes never make it to a real game. They vegetate on their couches or recliners while watching televised games. If they are college football watchers, they'll be glued to the set all day Saturday. If they're NFL fans, Sunday is their day. A hardy few spend all weekend watching football. These fans aren't hard to spot. Just look for the bleary-eyed chunk of lard with the catsup stain running down its sweatshirt. Usually, their chairs will be surrounded by empty bottles, snack sacks, containers of chip dip, and dried remains of day-old sandwiches. None of these fans is really too poor to make it to a game; they are just too lazy. You'll never find the couch potato at any kind of game.

Die-hard fans, fair-weather fans, and couch-potato fans have just two common traits. They are all a little crazy, and they are all sure that everyone else has his or her priorities mixed up. The next time you go to a game, try to classify the different types of fans. Just remember, the couch potato won't be there.

DISCUSS

1. What is the thesis of Eric's essay?
2. What is the single principle of classification used in this essay?
3. Eric could have found a fourth or fifth category to add to his essay. Why do you suppose he didn't?
4. What do you think of Eric's transitions as he leads you from one group of football fans to the next? Are they good? Why?
5. How has Eric included a personal element of persuasion in his essay? Explain.

ACT

Write an essay in which you classify people, places, ideas, or objects into clear groupings. Remember the importance of including a thesis statement in your introduction. Also, plan the structure of your essay carefully, keeping in mind the guidelines for preparing and developing the classification essay.

You may use one of the following subjects or, if you prefer, develop one of your own. Be sure to narrow the subject so that it is appropriate for a 600 to 700 word essay.

Television comedians	Rock bands
Video jockeys	People at a concert
Cashiers in discount stores	Ambition
Parents	Weekends
Summer jobs	Vacations
Elderly drivers	Horror movies

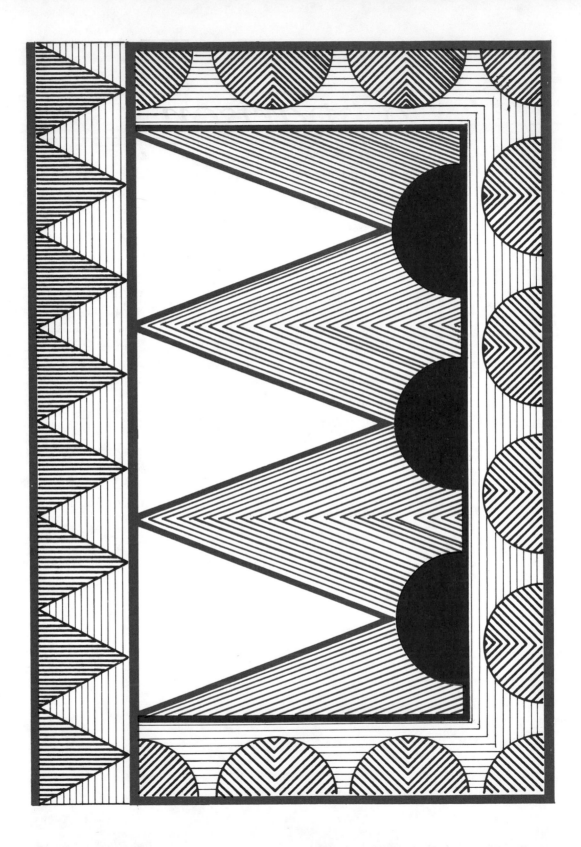

Comparison and Contrast

Bickvanh Cam stared into her lunch tray, obviously lost in thought and ignoring her taco salad. She didn't notice Jerry crossing the cafeteria toward her table, and when he set his tray down heavily, she gave a startled jump and smiled up at him.

"So, have you scheduled your senior interview with your counselor yet, Bik?"

"Jerry, I hate to even think about going in there. Ms. Morrison is going to want me to make a commitment about next year, and I really can't make up my mind."

"What's the problem? You've been accepted by your first and second choice colleges, and either of them would be great for you. I'd think you'd feel as if you're all set."

"It's not that easy. In fact, getting accepted by both Grinnell and the state university just complicates my life. At least, if one of them had turned me down, I wouldn't have to make the choice."

Jerry popped a french fry into his mouth and grinned. "I should have such problems."

"It's no joke. My parents aren't much help either. They'd like to see me settle it pretty quickly. They mean to be helpful, but they aren't going to make the decision for me, and there are too many variables."

"What do you mean?"

"Well, the state university has a lot of advantages, but, to be honest, I'm a little afraid that I'd get lost in a school that size. Being on a campus with thirty thousand other students sounds exciting, but it's a little overwhelming, too. I want to be more than just a number in some professor's huge class."

Jerry picked up a huge chili dog and inspected it carefully all the time he was talking. "I wouldn't worry. The idea that a small school can give you more individual attention is just propaganda they use to attract students. If you don't get the help you need, you can be part of a crowd in the private schools, too. I think the individual professor makes the real difference, and he or she might just as easily be teaching at the state university."

Bickvanh nodded. "Well, I know that, but I'm still a little nervous. Another thing is that my sister said the university might put me on a more direct track for law school. Grinnell has a good pre-law program, and they say that almost all of their graduates get into the law school they want, but I suppose the university background might be helpful."

"I don't see how that should mean anything," Jerry said. "It sounds good, but my mother went to a small college, and she had no trouble getting into medical school. And that was twenty years ago. Besides, weren't you talking about how you'd like to try out for the volleyball team? Wouldn't you have a better chance of playing at a smaller school?"

"You know, you're not a lot of help. Now you've given me two reasons to choose Grinnell and another reason to choose the university. The more I think about it, the more confused I get."

Jerry asked, "What about the ROTC program? I know the university has that, and you'd said it would help with expenses. Does Grinnell have ROTC?"

"No, they don't."

"How do the costs compare? Doesn't Grinnell cost at least twice as much?"

Bickvanh said, "Not when you figure in the financial help they'll give me. But I'd have to borrow some, and I hate to start doing that right away. It will be bad enough going into debt for law school." She hesitated a moment, and continued, "Unless I went through ROTC and let the military pay for law school."

Bickvanh closed her eyes, shook her head, and continued, "And I'm not sure I want to think about it any more. Now do you see why I've put off scheduling the senior interview? Ms. Morrison is going to think I can't make a decision, and maybe she's right. I really don't know what to do."

Jerry finally put his chili dog down and looked directly at Bickvanh. "Bik, you're always the logical one in humanities class. Every time someone starts to get emotional, you always tell him to cool down and think about the information he has. Why don't you just do the same?"

When Bickvanh gave him a disgusted look, Jerry surged ahead. "Make yourself a chart of all the advantages and disadvantages of the university. Then do the same for Grinnell. I bet you'll find that they're similar in a lot of ways, too. So far you've concentrated on the contrast between big and small. But a lot of what you want, you could get at either. That should make the choice less scary."

She nodded her head, but still sounded a little hesitant. "Okay. That way, maybe I could at least keep all the factors in mind. Sometimes I feel like I'm going to have an anxiety attack."

"You could make as logical a comparison as possible. Maybe it will make the choice seem a little less confusing."

"I suppose you're right. That's probably the only way I'll ever make a decision. I'm certainly not getting anywhere this way."

Looking relieved, Jerry said, "And I'm not getting anywhere with my lunch. Can we eat now?"

Bickvanh is about to use a common approach to life's tough choices. She's going to compare and contrast the major characteristics of the options she has available. When she has them all written out, she should be able to make the most intelligent decision possible. You have undoubtedly used the same method many times. *Compare* and *contrast* are commonly used terms in the essay questions your teachers use to test your understanding. For instance, you might have been asked to "Compare the British and American monetary systems," or "Contrast the military preparedness of the North with that of the South."

The comparison and contrast questions your teachers have given you in English or social studies tests are not artificial situations intended to twist your mind. In fact, using comparison and contrast is one of the most common methods of finding answers to life's choices. People compare and contrast colleges, cars, careers, and advertising claims. They think about the similarities and differences between athletic teams, vacation spots, employers, movies, and candidates for public office. As a result, comparison and contrast is also one of the most common kinds of writing tasks.

Because it is so common, comparison and contrast is not difficult to use. You do, however, need to consider several factors before actually writing a comparison and contrast essay, especially which of the two, comparison or contrast, you should use.

Comparison or Contrast?

The question of whether to concentrate on similarities or on differences depends almost entirely on the purpose of your essay. In some situations, you may serve your purpose best by emphasizing all the ways two things stand apart from one another. In others, you may feel the need to show that there is almost no difference between the two. Another time, your intention may not be to take sides but only to show as complete a picture as possible, and to include all the information you have available. Your purpose will determine your emphasis.

Contrast

If you were an advertising copywriter trying to sell a Cadillac sedan, you would probably want to show all the ways Cadillac is superior to the competition. You would talk about interior comfort, roominess, and quiet. You would mention elegant styling, fine bodywork, and a tradition of excellence. If this model has antilock brakes, you make a big point of their superiority. The standard sound system and the comfort-control system will both be a big part of your advertising.

If you were trying to sell an expensive computer, you would want your prospective buyer to understand how your product was better than anything the competition had for sale. You would talk about the massive memory, user friendliness, speed, and versatility. If your product can be used for word processing, creating database programs, and doing spreadsheet work, you will make a big point of those facts, especially if your software is superior to that of the competition. If your computer is being used in a lot of schools, and students will be familiar with it, those points, too, are worth mentioning.

On the other hand, what do you do if you are the copywriter for a four-door Chevrolet? Or even a comparatively inexpensive electronic typewriter?

Comparison

What you do when you are the less-expensive, maybe less-appealing, competition is show all the ways you compare favorably with the more-appealing product. In other words, you show all the things you have in common with the Cadillac, the IBM, or the Apple.

The Chevrolet advertisement may never mention more expensive cars, but it will point out that Chevrolet has more interior leg room than most cars its size. The upholstery has a real leather look, and the car has sound insulation added this year for a quieter ride. Not only was the body style developed by the same people that produced the Cadillac, but the Chevrolet carries the same engine and powertrain warranty as the Cadillac.

Nobody has said they are identical, but the two cars have a lot in common.

An advertisement for a Smith-Corona electronic typewriter is going to point out many ways the less-expensive product resembles a computer being used as a word processor. It has an electronic display window so you can see what you have typed, it has a built-in electronic spelling dictionary, and it has a memory that will hold your writing for several days. There is bidirectional printing, automatic centering, easy correction, and several other features that give you word-processing capabilities. This is not a complete word-processing program, such as you might get with the IBM or the Apple computer, but the advertising will point out that you get many similar features for a lot less money.

Combination

There may be times when your purpose is not to take sides, or show why one choice is superior to the other. Sometimes, you simply want to show as complete a picture as possible and include all the information you have available. In fact, you may not have decided which of the two is superior. Your whole purpose may be to organize your information so that you can make a choice.

The conversation between Jerry and Bickvanh illustrates that type of situation. When Bickvanh makes her list of advantages and disadvantages of the two schools, she will not be trying to sell either school. She just wants to get all her facts organized so that she can make an intelligent, informed choice. In that case, she will want to show both the advantages and disadvantages of the state university, and it will be just as important that she include all the advantages and disadvantages of Grinnell. She needs to consider all the possibilities.

A moment ago, you were picturing yourself as an advertising writer for cars, computers, and an electronic typewriter. Now, switch roles. Picture yourself as the consumer. If you are going to spend thousands of dollars for a computer system, you want to know everything about it. Not just what it will do, but what its advantages will be for you. Do you need all those capabilities? If you are going to spend several hundred dollars for the electronic typewriter, you want to know more than how it resembles a word processor. You also want to think about what it won't do. What features might you be used to on your school's computers that you won't get on the electronic typewriter? Is it worth the difference? Do you need all the computer features, and how much are those features worth to you?

Only by examining comparisons as well as contrasts will you be able to make an informed choice.

SUMMARY

When you compare, you take two people, ideas, or things and show their similarities. When you contrast, you show the differences between them. Whether you should emphasize the similarities or the differences will depend on what you hope to accomplish with your essay.

If your purpose is to show that one political candidate's ideas about drug law enforcement are much superior to those of her opponent, you will concentrate on showing the differences between candidates. If you feel that neither candidate has anything original to say about the topic, you would emphasize the similarities. If you simply want to inform your readers, without taking a stand, you would try to find a balance by pointing out ways in which their ideas are similar (how to handle dealers and smugglers) and other ways in which they are different (drug testing in the workplace).

DISCUSS

1. In what kinds of situations should a writer emphasize similarities? Give a specific example.
2. When might concentrating on differences seem more appropriate? Give a specific example.
3. In some cases, the writer may be wise to spend approximately the same amount of time on similarities and differences. Explain how this could happen. Describe a specific situation.

ACT

For each of the essay topics below, tell whether you would use comparison, contrast, or a combination of the two. Explain your answer.

1. You are a salesperson trying to sell a ten-speed bicycle.
2. You are the customer trying to decide whether to buy a five-speed or a ten-speed bicycle.

3. You are trying to decide whether you should go on vacation to Washington, D.C., or to San Francisco.
4. You are trying to explain to a friend why you believe religious discrimination can be even harder to deal with than racial discrimination.
5. You are trying to convince your friend that eating in the school cafeteria is a smarter choice than going out to McDonald's.
6. You are trying to show why going to a small high school or going to a large high school will give you an almost identical preparation for college.
7. You are trying to show that either the large school or the small school gives the student a distinct advantage.

FOR YOUR JOURNAL

People are not always the way they seem, even if most of them would never intentionally try to deceive. Almost everyone reacts to stress by adjusting his or her behavior to the situation.

You are probably relaxed and informal with your friends and family. If you were to interview for a job, however, you would present another side of your personality, and your behavior might be almost unrecognizable. This is not being two-faced; it's adjusting to what is appropriate for the occasion.

But everyone knows someone whose change in behavior seems less innocent, and it's interesting to speculate about what motivates these people. Do they really think they are fooling anyone? At times, a person you don't know well may seem so perfect that you wonder what the other side is like. For instance, sometimes it's fun to imagine what a famous film or television personality might really be like when off-camera.

In your journal, contrast the way three or four well-known personalities appear in public with the way you imagine they might act in private. For example, you could describe some famous movie star promoting animal rights on the Johnny Carson Show, and then describe what she might say to the host during a commercial.

Later, you might imagine an actor being obnoxious and picking fights in front of the camera, but then becoming timid and apologetic when a commercial comes on. What do you suppose these people are really like?

The Thesis Statement

The thesis statement of a comparison and contrast essay presents a special problem and a special opportunity. The thesis statement is a problem to some writers because they have a tendency to act as if the purpose of comparison and contrast is limited to showing similarities and differences. The similarities and differences are not the purpose; they are the method by which you accomplish a larger purpose.

The thesis statement is an opportunity to make clear the real meaning of your comparison and contrast. While it is possible to write a comparison and contrast essay that is strictly informative, perfectly balanced, and refuses to take sides, more often your purpose will be to support an argument. In other words, you will be writing not just to show similarities or differences but to show what those similarities and differences mean to you. You'll be expressing an opinion.

For instance, if your essay shows all the differences between the service departments at two car dealerships, chances are you have a purpose. Most likely, you want to convince your reader that only one of those dealerships deserves his or her business. "Bernie's BMW has a much more dependable service department than does Willisonne Imports."

On the other hand, when you show all the similarities among the merchandise offered at an exclusive, expensive department store and the merchandise sold at a discount store, you are probably trying to make the point that the discount store may be a logical place to do a lot of shopping. "While Discount City may not have all the trendy neon displays found at Millazzo's, the merchandise they handle is very similar."

In fact, even if you plan to show all the similarities and differences, and have no intention of choosing one object, idea, or person over the other, you probably have a specific purpose in mind. Even the statement "There is no way to be certain whether Rocky Marciano or Muhammad Ali was the better boxer" expresses an opinion and invites comparison of the two men.

Clearly then, any comparison and contrast essay worth the time you put into it is a form of argument. The important thing is to decide beforehand what those similarities and differences mean so you so that you can write a meaningful thesis sentence. Avoid purely informative thesis sentences that say no more than

"There are a lot of differences between Hemingway and Faulkner." Instead, take a stand: "Hemingway relies more on the reader's imagination to fill in details than does Faulkner."

A final word on your thesis sentence. While there is no rule saying you must, your essay will be much easier to keep under control if you limit yourself to two objects, ideas, or persons. If you have good reason for doing so, three or more items can be compared and contrasted. But more than two can become unwieldy, and there is no reason to make things harder on yourself or on your reader.

SUMMARY

A comparison and contrast essay usually has a much larger purpose than simply showing how two things are alike or different. Generally, you will be writing to express an opinion about the significance of those similarities and differences. Be sure your thesis statement makes that opinion clear. Avoid the purely informative thesis statement.

DISCUSS

1. How is the thesis statement of a comparison and contrast essay particularly challenging?
2. In what way would it be accurate to say that showing similarities and differences is not the true purpose of a comparison and contrast essay?

ACT

For five of the comparison and contrast topics listed below, write a thesis sentence that reveals a specific purpose for examining the two objects, ideas, or people.
1. Chicago Cubs / St. Louis Cardinals
2. Rome / Paris
3. American Revolution / French Revolution
4. Going steady / Staying uncommitted
5. Medical school / Law school
6. Living in the city / living in the country
7. Cable television / free television
8. Discipline on the job / discipline in school
9. Two cars
10. Two movies
11. Two employers
12. Two friends
13. Two theories

14. Two philosophies
15. Two political parties

Organization

The possibility of confusion always exists in a comparison and contrast essay. Since you will be discussing two different objects, persons, or ideas, and possibly dividing your discussion between several similarities and differences, even the most uncomplicated of comparison and contrast essays will have more elements than you are used to handling. It is important to use a simple structure that will reduce the chance of confusion as much as possible. In this essay, even more than in others, outlining is essential.

With the comparison and contrast essay, there are two common plans of organization, the opposing pattern and the alternating pattern.

Opposing Pattern

In the opposing pattern, the entire first half of an essay is devoted to the first of your topics. The second half is devoted entirely to the second topic. For instance, if you were writing about two kinds of talk shows, the "Oprah Winfrey Show" and the "Arsenio Hall Show," you would tell everything you have to say about Oprah Winfrey in the first half. Arsenio Hall would be covered in the second half.

The following outline illustrates how you could organize the opposing pattern.

Thesis: The "Arsenio Hall Show" is much more straightforward about its purpose than is the "Oprah Winfrey Show."

    I. The "Oprah Winfrey Show"
       A. Role of the host
       B. Role of the guests
       C. Topics discussed
       D. Audience participation
       E. Purpose of the show

II. The "Arsenio Hall Show"
A. Role of the host
B. Role of the guests
C. Topics discussed
D. Audience Participation
E. Purpose of the show

Notice that each subtopic under the "Oprah Winfrey Show" is also discussed under the "Arsenio Hall Show." Since this essay will point out differences between the two shows, it makes no sense to mention Oprah Winfrey's role as host if you have nothing to say about Arsenio Hall's role. Her role matters only in the way it can be contrasted with his role.

Also, remember that the first part of the essay covers all the subtopics in the same order as the second part covers those subtopics. Since audience participation and the purpose of the show complete the discussion of the "Oprah Winfrey Show," they should also come at the end of the "Arsenio Hall Show" segment.

This organizational pattern will allow your reader to receive a separate total impression of each show. It is probably the best choice for short papers with very few characteristics. However, if your paper is long, by the time the reader reaches the end some of your first points will have been forgotten. In that situation, consider the alternating pattern.

Alternating Pattern

The alternating pattern moves back and forth between its two topics. Instead of writing about Oprah Winfrey in the first half of the paper and Arsenio Hall in the second half, the writer swings back and forth between them throughout the paper. The following outline illustrates how you would organize the alternating pattern.

Thesis: The "Arsenio Hall Show" is much more straightforward about its purpose than the "Oprah Winfrey Show."
I. Role of the host
A. Oprah Winfrey
B. Arsenio Hall

   II. Role of the guests
      A. Oprah Winfrey
      B. Arsenio Hall

  III. Topics discussed
      A. Oprah Winfrey
      B. Arsenio Hall
  IV. Audience participation
      A. Oprah Winfrey
      B. Arsenio Hall
   V. Purpose of the show
      A. Oprah Winfrey
      B. Arsenio Hall

Since, in this pattern, topic sentences for each paragraph refer to the individual characteristics rather than the people being discussed, the alternating pattern works very well if emphasizing those characteristics is important to your purpose.

This pattern is also particularly useful when you have a large number of characteristics to cover. If you have eight or ten characteristics to discuss, and choose the opposing pattern, your reader could easily forget what you said about the earliest ones by the time you get back to them in the second half of the essay.

Since most of your essays are likely to be neither particularly long nor particularly short, the choice of which pattern to use will probably depend on another factor—your purpose. The pattern that's right for an essay is the one that allows you to achieve the emphasis you need to support your thesis. Additionally, since either pattern will cover the same information, the choice of which to use is often a matter of personal preference and a feeling for which works best with your set of circumstances.

SUMMARY

Using a highly structured pattern is important to the success of your comparison and contrast essay. The opposing pattern deals with all of the first topic in the first half of the essay, and all of the second topic in the second half. The alternating pattern swings back and forth between the two topics, describing each of them in its relationship with each of your subpoints. Usually, the opposing pattern works best for shorter papers, and the alternating pattern works best for longer papers.

DISCUSS

1. Why are having a structure and an outline important in the comparison and contrast essay?
2. Why is the opposing pattern usually most effective for shorter essays?
3. How does the alternating pattern emphasize the individual characteristics of the subjects being discussed?
4. Why is the purpose of your writing the most important factor in deciding which pattern to use?

ACT

!!

In the previous lesson of this chapter, you wrote five thesis sentences, each of which revealed a specific purpose for comparing two objects, ideas, or people. Select two of those thesis sentences and outline an essay you could write to compare and contrast the two elements. Use an opposing pattern for one of the outlines and an alternating pattern for the other. Be sure to select thesis sentences that seem appropriate for each pattern.

FOR YOUR JOURNAL

In his book *Writing with a Word Processor,* William Zinsser tells about learning to work with words on a screen after a lifetime of using pencil and paper. He never says that it seemed frustrating or impossible, only that he was reluctant at first to invest the time and energy necessary for learning the skill. After learning, he became so excited about the experience and his increased productivity that he felt everyone should try it. He writes in the tone of someone who has discovered a revolutionary, earth-shaking phenomenon.

That kind of excitement about a new way of performing an old task is something you may have experienced. If you have worked with a word processor, you may know what Zinsser was feeling. Even if you do not agree with him, you know that it is different from working with pencil and paper.

In your journal, compare and contrast your experience in finding a new way to perform some old job. You could write about a word processor. Or, if your school library has on-line computer research capabilities, compare that with the old way of locating information through the *Readers' Guide to Periodical Literature.* Compact disc technology is also giving some school libraries tremendous research capabilities. If you prefer, write about some labor-saving device around your house and how it has changed the way you do things.

Whatever you choose, be sure to think about all the results of the change. Especially, how does it affect the quality of your work? The quantity? Speed? Effort? What you expect of yourself? Are there any other results you may not have considered?

A Comparison and Contrast Essay

The following essay was written to show the writer's attitude toward a major change that took place in his life. Read the essay and answer the questions that follow.

Brad Remmert
Composition II
Ms. Webster
November 12, 19_____

Schoolboy Blues

In sophomore and junior years, my gauges read all systems go; now the red warning lights flicker constantly. I once worked for superior grades, participated in classes, and maintained a first-rate attitude. But this year, my attitude has shifted gears.

Until this year, I acted like a textbook student. I didn't talk to anyone in class because I figured my teacher would send me to the principal's office for detention. I couldn't handle the thought of a summons to the principal with all my classmates watching. When the teacher finished teaching, I started working on homework. In fact, I always managed my schedule so I wouldn't waste any time. My classroom grades reflected this attitude and effort, and I earned straight *A*'s.

Between classes I dashed for my next room because I didn't want a tardy. Tardiness ranked right up there with talking on my list of rules that didn't get broken. I also carried books for more than one class, so I wouldn't waste precious time fiddling with my locker combination. For me, promptness was essential.

When I got home from football practice, I worked to complete any assignments for the next day. I made sure that I never turned in assignments late, because I dreaded a lecture on the importance of punctuality. I usually didn't have to work for long because the homework assignments seemed light.

I carried a clean record for two years. Then, the tables suddenly turned. I found myself working on long homework assignments every night, becoming flustered, and falling behind. Once I had fallen behind on my work, I found my whole attitude changing.

Homework has affected the way I look at school. Now I space off and fall asleep during class because I know the homework will still be there even if I start on my assignments in class. Teachers usually allow no more than five or ten minutes to work in class, and by the time I put a heading on paper, it's time to leave. My in-class production has plummeted.

I try to use all of the allotted time between classes. Instead of rushing to my next class, I loiter in the hallways. Then, I stroll into class at the last second carrying little or nothing. Since I can't stand lugging around a stack of books, I try to take only the essentials. The essentials consist of a folder and a pen. That way, if I bump into any important people, they won't think I'm too brainy. You never know when you might see someone important.

I spend a lot of time before school trying to complete unfinished assignments. It's hard to play football and go to school at the same time. Practices take up a great deal of time, so some nights I do my most important work first and put the rest off until morning. Teachers seem to forget that football players don't get home until about six every night. I understand that teachers need to give homework, but the evening seems very short when you are tired and sore from a long practice.

I still strive for respectable grades, but my work ethic has changed tremendously, and my once well managed day is in chaos. Frequent homework assignments have caused me to become uninterested and unwilling to complete them. My fine-tuned machine needs a trip to the repair shop.

DISCUSS

1. What pattern, opposing or alternating, did Brad use? Why do you suppose he chose this pattern?
2. What is Brad's thesis sentence? What does it suggest about the significance of his change?
3. Write a brief outline of Brad's essay. Does he treat the major characteristics of his behavior in both parts of the essay?
4. In what way does Brad use the paper to inform or persuade? What is he saying about the importance of his "burnout"?
5. How did Brad tie his introduction and conclusion together? Is it an effective device in this essay? Why? Why not?

ACT

At the beginning of this chapter, Bickvanh Cam was about to take the first steps that could have led to an essay about how she chose a college. She was going to list all the significant characteristics, good and bad, of the college and the university she was considering.

Using comparison and contrast, write an essay that shows how you made some significant decision. You may, if you choose, write about a decision you are in the process of making or one that you think you might have to make in the future. If you write about a future decision, you can use a topic of your choice or a topic from the following list.

1. A choice between a class you could use for college or one that will almost guarantee a better grade
2. A choice between careers
3. A choice between college majors
4. A choice between working when you go to college or borrowing money so you can concentrate on studying
5. A choice between going directly into college or taking time off for the military
6. A choice between marrying now or waiting until later

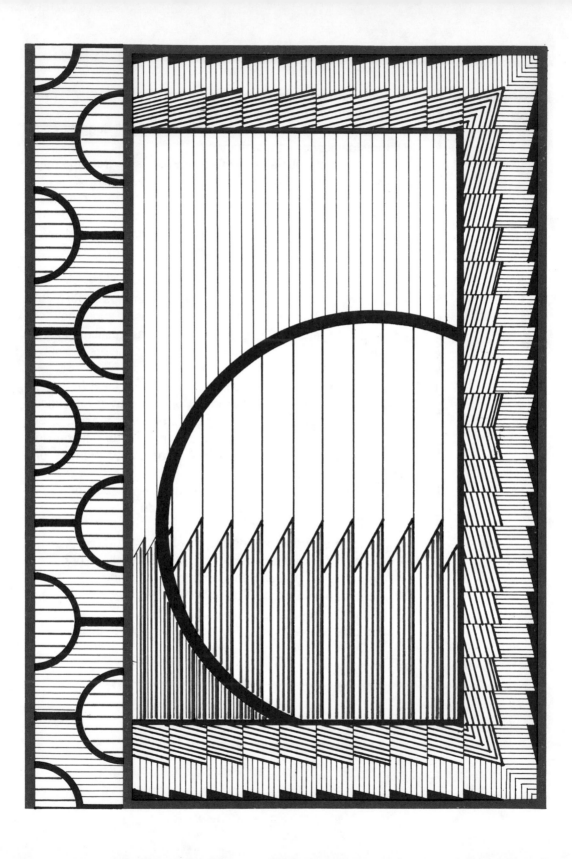

9

The Inductive Argument

Originally, the March of Dimes was called the National Foundation for Infantile Paralysis. Its fund-raising campaigns made possible the research that led to development of the first successful polio vaccine by Dr. Jonas Salk and, a few years later, an even more successful oral vaccine by Dr. Albert Sabin. These vaccines were so effective that they put the National Foundation for Infantile Paralysis out of its original business. In the year before the Salk vaccine was available, 60,000 cases of polio were reported, mostly among younger people. Now the disease is almost unheard of. The National Foundation has changed its name to the March of Dimes, and today it finances research and professional education for the prevention of birth defects.

Naturally, the polio vaccines had to be tested before they could be pronounced safe and effective. The Sabin vaccine is a good example of how that was done. The first step was to be certain that inoculation would not cause the paralysis that made polio so horrible. Rhesus monkeys, physiologically very similar to humans, were used for the first tests. When extensive testing showed no effect on the central nervous systems of the monkeys, Dr. Sabin and others volunteered to have the vaccine tested on themselves. After that, field tests were conducted in which thousands of young people took the vaccine orally. Those thousands of individual cases eventually led to the conclusion that the vaccine was not only harmless but was truly effective in preventing the paralytic form of the disease.

All that testing, thousands upon thousands of individual experiments in which the vaccine acted predictably, was a practical application of a logical principle used in all scientific research. The principle is that, if you observe enough individual experiments that produce the same result, you can safely predict what will happen in the future. This principle of logic is called *inductive reasoning,* and it has an equally useful application to your own writing.

Arguing Inductively

Every time you write an essay, you go through a series of steps. These include writing a thesis sentence and brainstorming ideas to support that thesis. Imagine what kind of evidence you would need to support the following thesis sentences.

-Motorcycle riders who have taken a Motorcycle Safety Foundation Experienced Rider Course have fewer accidents than those who have not had that instruction.

-When oppressed minority groups use peaceful resistance, they achieve their goals more quickly.

-People from different religious backgrounds who plan to marry should first get counseling.

-Required high school driver education courses have made young drivers much safer than they used to be.

-Participation in extracurricular activities leads to better grades.

Each of these statements is a generalization considered true by a large number of people. It would not be surprising, however, if many people disagreed. And all of the statements would be difficult to prove to everyone's satisfaction.

For instance, you undoubtedly could provide many facts and examples showing how driver education courses have made young drivers safer over the years. But there are so many variables that attributing improved safety records entirely to driver education seems unwise. The number of miles driven by students, new safety features in cars, improved highways, and more accurate methods of reporting accidents have all affected safety records. Consequently, *proving* your thesis is nearly impossible.

What you must do, then, is gather a reasonable amount of evidence to support your generalization about driver education courses and show how that evidence logically leads to your conclusion. If you can show that a large number of students drive more safely because of training they received in school, you can show by implication that requiring driver education courses has, on the whole, made young drivers much safer than they used to be. What is true of the parts is also true of the whole.

Logicians have a term for the moment when you decide that you have examined enough evidence to safely conclude that additional examination would yield identical results. It's called the *inductive leap.* Because you are making the inductive leap over any remaining evidence, there is always a slim chance of error but, if you study your evidence carefully, the leap is warranted.

You might follow a similar process if you wanted to make an important purchase, such as a car, and were considering a particular make and model. You could read *Consumer Reports,* get recommendations from friends, and talk to a mechanic. No one of these sources will be able to make up your mind for you, but together they can offer observations, facts, and experiences that will help you generalize about whether this should be a good car for you. If the *Consumer Reports* staff's research shows it to be a good car, and your mechanic is impressed with it, and your friends have heard mostly good things about it, you would probably be reasonably safe in generalizing that this is a good car.

This process of coming to conclusions about the whole based on observations of facts and examples is a form of the same reasoning process used by medical researchers. You examine available evidence, consider that evidence as representative of the whole, and generalize that the whole would be a continuation of the sample. While the name of that process, induction, may be new to you, the process itself is an everyday occurrence. You have done it for years, and so has the rest of humankind.

In fact, the process is so natural that Aristotle, a Greek philosopher, teacher, and scientist who lived almost twenty-five hundred years ago, included induction when he taught about reasoning processes by which people should be able to understand their world. Philosophers Francis Bacon, David Hume, John Stuart Mill, and Charles Sanders Peirce all worked from the principles of induction. Even Sir Arthur Conan Doyle, best known for his Sherlock Holmes stories, made frequent use of inductive reasoning. In fact, inductive reasoning has been studied and used so successfully throughout history that sometimes it is easy to forget it has a major drawback.

By its nature, inductive reasoning does not lead to certain knowledge. When you make the mental leap from examining your sample to assuming the sample represents all others of its kind, you create the possibility of error. For instance, when you gathered information about the car you wanted to buy, there was plenty of room for error. *Consumer Reports* liked the car, but other testing agencies might have disagreed. Your mechanic had good experience with it, but that's only one mechanic. Your friends were impressed, too, but their experience is limited. If you don't examine every single example, there is the possibility of an exception. So, in spite of its popularity, induction is a risky business.

Still, you must use it. The alternative is to learn nothing from your experiences and gain nothing from information you have available. What you must do is learn and follow some guidelines for reliable induction.

SUMMARY

Research scientists sometimes use a form of logic called inductive reasoning. They gather information in the form of experiments and reports, examine that evidence, and try to draw generalizations from it. They operate on the principle that what is true of the parts is true of the whole.

You can use inductive reasoning in your essays. The process involves finding a reasonable number of examples and showing that what is true of your examples is likely to be true for all other examples.

DISCUSS

1. Define inductive reasoning. Give an example of how it is used.
2. What is the inductive leap?
3. In what sense is induction a dangerous process of reasoning?
4. Why is inductive reasoning necessary in spite of the possibility of error?

ACT

Choose two of the following topics. For each, describe how you would go about gathering evidence that would support that point of view. What facts would you need? Where would you find the evidence? How many examples would you need to make your point convincing?

1. Americans depend too much on their cars.
2. Recent reforms have strengthened (or weakened) American education.
3. Gun control laws are (are not) necessary.
4. Excessive absence seriously affects a student's performance in class.
5. Seat belt laws help reduce the cost of car insurance.

FOR YOUR JOURNAL

Saturday morning cartoons seem to be a grand old custom for American children. It's likely that most teenagers and a great number of adults have pleasant memories of the hours spent in front of the television set every Saturday morning. Not everyone, however, feels that this custom is harmless or that the intentions of the broadcasters are above suspicion.

One criticism concerns the commercials shown during that time period. No one should be surprised that the commercials are aimed at children, and that these commercials run heavily to toys and sugar-coated breakfast cereals. Critics say that children are not capable of understanding the commercials in the same way that adults would, and regulations should control what is being sold and how it is described. Defenders of the programming say that children are much more capable of making rational choices than they are given credit for.

It is probably safe to say that not all children are equally perceptive, but no one seems to agree on just how gullible they are. In your journal, write down your feelings about what a person could do to study the problem. Just how much of what children see and hear can they understand? If faced with the prospect of limiting the advertisers' right to persuade children, how would a lawmaker find evidence to show just how susceptible children are to advertising? Who could supply that information, and how would you get it?

Reliability of Inductive Reasoning

Inductive reasoning involves generalizing without having examined every sample. Consequently, the possibility of error always exists. In spite of this, you can set standards that will make error much less likely. The long tradition of inductive reasoning, beginning with early philosophers and continuing into the present, is a great advantage. The pitfalls of induction were discovered long ago, and you can learn all you need to know from other's mistakes. The following suggestions, when followed carefully, make inductive arguments extremely reliable.

Evidence Must Be True

Though this suggestion seems obvious, at least two problems do crop up. The first is the possibility of deliberate distortion. Writers have been known to mislead readers or make up evidence to support a thesis. You need look no further than politics or advertising to realize that readers need to be alert. To be blunt, money and ambition create temptations that some people can't resist.

Usually, though, it is safe to assume that a writer who uses inductive reasoning will do so honestly. Most people prefer being honest, and even if they didn't, the stakes are too high to risk a lie. It is no exaggeration to say that the professional writer who lies is risking his or her career. In these days when people accept information at face value, a writer's reputation for honesty is crucial. It would be foolish to falsify information that can be checked easily, and the availability of information today makes almost anything easy to verify.

How does this apply to your writing? That's where the second problem can arise. The writer must be scrupulously careful. Often, poor inductive reasoning is a result not of dishonesty but of carelessness. You must be certain of your facts. You would also be wise to identify your sources so that the reader knows your information is reliable. If you use information that seems surprising or may be questioned by your readers, offer evidence or cite a trusted authority. Remember that your conclusions are only as reliable as the support you offer.

Evidence Must Be Gathered Impartially

Forming a tentative hypothesis is normal and undoubtedly a good idea. Before you can gather meaningful evidence, you must have an idea of what you expect to find. But, since this hypothesis is formed before the research begins, it can be dangerous. The writer may then fall into the trap of gathering only information that supports the hypothesis and overlooking, or ignoring, information that contradicts it.

Strictly speaking, true induction begins with a clear slate, gathers all information available, and then weighs the evidence to see what conclusions seem appropriate. In reality, there is a great temptation to notice only evidence that supports the writer's hypothesis. This is not necessarily a result of dishonesty, but comes from a human trait of seeing what serves the immediate purpose. People notice those examples that justify their opinions, and easily overlook those that contradict them. For your part, be aware and be careful.

Evidence Must Be Representative

The evidence used to support your conclusion must represent a true cross-section of the group you are generalizing about. This means that your sample must be chosen thoughtfully.

In selecting your sample, you can take either of two approaches. Ideally, you would select your representative sample very deliberately. For instance, for an essay about student reactions to your school's new policy on unexcused absences, you would get the most accurate information if you interviewed students from each grade level. You would also want the opinions of students from various social groups and extracurricular groups. You might even want to be sure you get the opinions of students with a cross-section of grade-point averages. As much as possible, you would include representatives of every student group.

Sometimes, however, it is impossible to control your sample well enough to be sure that you have a true cross-section. In that case, the next best procedure is to choose your sample entirely by chance. From a student list, pick every tenth name. Or select every tenth student who uses the drinking fountain. You could even pick students out of the crowd as they leave the building in the afternoon.

Even the chance method, however, has pitfalls. If various groups in your school tend to cluster in one part of the building, be aware of that and adjust accordingly. For example, if a large number of athletes habitually use the door nearest the gym, be aware of this and don't get all of your opinions at that door. If your school assigns lockers so that one hallway seems to be full of sophomores, don't get all of your opinions at the drinking fountain in that hallway. Be aware of any situations that might make the opinions less representative of the whole, and adjust your procedure.

Evidence Must Support the Conclusion

The evidence used to arrive at your conclusion might be 100 percent true and gathered so carefully as to be irrefutable. But if you don't establish a direct connection between the evidence and the conclusion, your task is incomplete and error is likely.

A newspaper reporter in one midwestern city heard rumors that a lot of downtown merchants were closing their stores. He decided to do a little research. A visit to the business section showed that the rumors were based in fact. What had once been a thriving collection of retail stores was deteriorating to the point where it now looked like the beginning of a ghost town. Many stores were closed and one of them had windows broken out. Several storefronts were boarded up. A quick count revealed that three small department stores, a drugstore, and twelve specialty shops had closed within a four-block area. Streets that a year earlier had been bustling with activity were nearly deserted.

From this evidence, gathered first-hand by walking around the neighborhood for two hours, talking to a few pedestrians, and counting abandoned buildings, the writer concluded that the town's retail trade was dying. According to the story he wrote that day, economic doom was inevitable.

And then the embarrassment began. Letters, most of them from local merchants, flew in. A few agreed with the gloomy conclusion, but most were from area merchants who had moved within the last nine months to one of the new, fully enclosed, heated, and air conditioned malls on the edge of town. The writers pointed out how their new locations provided plenty of free parking and a comfortable social center that customers seemed to enjoy. Sales were up. While the negative effect on the downtown area was unfortunate, the reporter's conclusion that economic disaster had struck the merchants was completely off the mark. They were doing quite well, thank you very much. From the point of view of the few remaining downtown merchants, business was bad, but those who moved had found greener pastures.

The reporter's evidence was 100 percent true. Forty percent of the merchants had left the traditional business area. But his conclusion about business conditions was not an inevitable conclusion. When you write, be sure that your evidence really does lead to your conclusion.

Evidence Must Be Plentiful

A common accusation from someone who disagrees with your conclusion might be "Those are just exceptions" or "You're not looking at the whole picture."

You know that induction, by its nature, means you don't have to examine every possible instance. That's the beauty of induction. You can reach dependable conclusions without having to look at every example. But you can also sense immediately that there must be a minimum. How much evidence is enough to support your conclusion?

Statisticians use a term that is useful in discussing how much evidence is enough. Instead of referring to those who are being generalized about as "everybody," "the group," or "the whole bunch," they refer to the total from which a sample is taken as "the population."

Two basic rules govern how large a sample (the part studied) should be taken from a given population (the whole about which you will be reaching a conclusion):

1. The larger the population, the larger the sample you must examine.
2. The smaller the population, the greater the percentage of that population you must examine.

To understand this, imagine that you have a swimming pool filled with one million marbles. The marbles come in three colors: blue, red, and green. But the numbers of blue, red, and green marbles are not equal, and you cannot determine what the distribution is by sight alone. You could separate all one million marbles into three piles and count each pile, but that would take too long. Besides, you know that a randomly picked sample of marbles should allow you to determine the percentage of blue, red, and green in the swimming pool. How many marbles must you pull out of the pool before you can make an inductive leap and state with certainty how many marbles of each color are in the pool?

You will have to make your own determination because there are no set rules to cover the situation. It seems reasonable to believe, however, that if you used a pail to randomly scoop 10,000 marbles out of the pool, and counted 4,500 blue, 3,500 red, and 2,000 green marbles, you could say with reasonable certainty that the entire pool has *about* 450,000 blue marbles, 350,000 red marbles, and 200,000 green marbles.

Remember, though the 10,000 marbles will make three very large piles and will take quite a while to count, these piles only make up 1 percent of the one million marbles you are generalizing about. If you are generalizing about a large population, you must examine a large sample, even though the percentage is small.

Now, suppose that instead of a swimming pool full of marbles, you had a washtub full of only one thousand marbles—again, red, green, and blue. Would anyone really expect to reach a supportable conclusion about their distribution by picking only ten marbles—that is, 1 percent—out of the tub? With the smaller population, you would need to sample a much larger percentage of the marbles, even though the total number would be nowhere near what you sampled from the swimming pool. A small population requires that the sample be a greater percentage of the population.

Put more simply:
Large population equals large sample; small percentage
Small population equals small sample; large percentage.

How do readers know if you have followed these guidelines? Is it necessary to remind your readers about how fair your research has been? Of course not.

You don't have to use valuable space justifying yourself. Within reason, show where the information came from, but don't go into great detail. You don't expect it from other writers, and no one expects it of you. It would make pretty boring reading and, besides, people still operate on the principle that others are trustworthy.

You should be sure, however, to give a reasonable number of examples and phrase your conclusions in terms of probability rather than certainty. You wouldn't, for example, claim to have proved that your swimming pool has a specific number of red marbles in it. "It has about 350,000 red marbles" is a safer pronouncement.

 SUMMARY

Because inductive reasoning involves a possibility of error, you should follow five guidelines for the use of evidence. The evidence must be true, gathered impartially, representative of the whole, supportive of the conclusion, and plentiful. As a writer, you are responsible for adhering to these guidelines, but you do not need to mention them in your essay. You should remember, however, that failure to keep them in mind can lead to embarrassing mistakes.

 DISCUSS

1. Assuming that you would not lie, how does the "Evidence must be true" guideline affect your writing?
2. How can a writer be certain that his or her evidence is impartial?

3. Explain the two approaches to being certain that your sample is representative of the whole population.
4. Explain the importance of showing a direct connection between your evidence and your conclusion.
5. Name and explain the two rules that govern how large your sample must be.

ACT

Each of the following generalizations makes use of inductive reasoning. Study the evidence in each one and tell how reliable the conclusion is likely to be. If one of the rules of inductive reasoning is violated, point out and explain the problem.

1. I see from this week's edition of *National Tattler* that the addition of fluoride to drinking water has caused thousands of deformed children to be born in the last ten years. I guess we're going to have to outlaw fluoride use.
2. A survey of our school's athletes shows that we need more pep assemblies.
3. The school's camera club has been trying to boost membership, mostly without success. Monica Stitch suggested that they would have better luck if they held meetings in the evening instead of right after school when so many students are involved in other activities. The other members shouted her down, though, saying that evening meetings would cause too many other conflicts.
4. The principal of this school is afraid to discipline everyone equally. Jeff Brown, the football player, has been absent twelve times this semester and nothing has been done about it.
5. Ms. Conner must be a terrific teacher. No matter what time of day you walk by, her class is absolutely silent.

FOR YOUR JOURNAL

Americans have been accused of being a nation of consumers. While that may be unfair, most people do spend at least some time thinking about things they would like to have. For one person, it may be a new camera; for another, it might be a new car. The distinguishing characteristic for most of these dream purchases is that they are beyond the limit of a person's budget. When you finally buy your dream camera or car or stereo, you will have put a lot of thought into it. And even if you never get it, it's fun to dream.

What is your dream purchase? Don't limit yourself by reality. If money were no concern, what one consumer item would you like to have?

In your journal, explain what makes it the best of its kind. What are the features that, added together, make this camera or car or whatever the best a person could buy? Include all the data, specifications, characteristics, and even opinions of your friends that help convince you that this is the best.

Gathering Your Own Evidence

Writing an essay based on inductive reasoning is a straightforward, five-step process.

1. Choose a topic you are interested in.
2. State a tentative opinion you believe can be supported by evidence.
3. Gather the evidence.
4. Evaluate the evidence. Evidence that points to a different conclusion may alter your opinion. You will still have a thesis backed by concrete evidence.
5. Organize your evidence into an effective argument.

You'll find many topics appropriate for applying inductive reasoning and for which the supporting evidence is readily available.

For instance, suppose you want to write a paper supporting the statement "Sexism is a major problem in our school" or "Our school has dealt effectively with the problem of sexism." You have a great deal of easily obtainable information. Much of it you probably already know, and most of the rest is close at hand.

Remember that your hypothesis should be held only tentatively. You may personally feel strongly on the issue, but you should be ready to alter your opinion if the facts contradict your opinion. Be fair. Until you have honestly searched for evidence of sexism or the lack of it, don't be surprised by anything you find.

The first step is to come up with pertinent questions. With a little thought you can answer some of them yourself, and with a little leg work, you can find authorities.

How many sports are available for boys' participation? How many for girls'? If there is a difference, why? How much money is spent on boys' athletics? On girls'? The information is a matter of public record, and your athletic director could answer those questions easily.

Do you have male cheerleaders? If you do, ask them how they are treated. If you don't, why not? Do the boys have a volleyball team? Do both girls and boys have track and cross-country teams? If you don't have all of these, are the existing sports opportunities evenly distributed?

Are student forum offices fairly evenly divided? How about representatives? If there is a difference, ask the faculty sponsor if this is a typical distribution for other years as well.

How many male students are enrolled in home economics classes? It's reasonable to expect that less than half will be boys, but just how many are there? On the other hand, how many girls are enrolled in industrial technology or shop classes? Anywhere near half? Twenty-five percent? Talk to some students who are in the minority in a female- or male-dominated class. How are they treated? Why did they enroll in these classes? You may even want to ask some other students if they have ever thought of enrolling in a "nontraditional" class and see what kind of reaction you get.

Talk to several teachers. Do the novels used in literature classes present an approximately equal number of male and female protagonists? If not, is there a good reason, or did it just happen without anyone's notice? Are male and female authors represented? Who takes upper-level math classes? For that matter, does your school have a reasonable balance of men and women teachers? These are the kinds of questions you could use to gather evidence during a typical school day.

As you are gathering evidence, keep in mind that evaluation of the facts is just as important as the information itself. No one has yet found a reliable way to measure common sense, but you will need to make some sound judgments about the evidence you find.

Does the fact that your school has no girls' football team mean sexism is a problem? Most people would say no. But do the girls have an alternative activity? Do you have a girls' volleyball team instead?

Does the fact that only 35 percent of the home economics students are boys prove the boys are being discouraged from taking home economics? Given past attitudes about what was suitable as a "girls' course" or "boys' course," 35 percent may be fairly high. Or maybe not. Exercising your judgment is always important. Don't expect to prove anything beyond the shadow of a doubt. Do expect to build a case that will support a reasonably limited thesis.

Once you have examined your evidence, you should be able to come to a sensible conclusion about the existence of sexism in your school. Since you are reasoning inductively, not conducting a year-long, exhaustive investigation of the topic, your results are best phrased conservatively. "Although progress has been made, a residue of sexism still clings to Hampton High School," or "Hampton High School seems to have dealt with most of its problems concerning sexism."

Your final step is to decide which evidence is most representative. Then, using all your essay-writing skills, arrange that evidence in an effective and convincing order.

In the following essay, Jenni Dohlman started with the tentative hypothesis that a book causing some controversy had literary and educational value that should override any objections to its content. A citizens' organization said the book contained objectionable language and had no value in the classroom. Jenni reread the book, searching for specific incidents and lessons that might support her feeling that it had real value. Rereading the book convinced her more than ever that the novel, *To Kill a Mockingbird,* taught important lessons about history and the nature of human relationships.

Jenni Dohlman
Composition II
Ms. Alberts
February 23, 19_____

It's a Sin to Kill a Mockingbird

The child, your child, sits and watches, unable to defend himself, as you take away a part of history. It is not his fault, nor is it yours, that the events, phrases, and philosophies in this book were common at one time. The book is a fictional but not untruthful way of portraying them. This novel, *To Kill a Mockingbird,* helps describe the depth of the prejudice felt in those times by blacks and whites alike, and banning this book from the classroom would be hiding history and depriving students of some important lessons.

It's true that the few instances of cursing and racial slurs are unpleasant and sometimes contemptible, but they are a part of the real world and not likely to be new to any high school students today. Oddly, almost none of the students I talked to remembered any cursing. Almost all of them remembered the racial insults but felt that those were a part of the times. Or that they were being used by the author as a method of characterizing the speakers. Students read the book for enjoyment and the educational experience, not to pick out the most offensive words they can find. Bad language or not, *To Kill a Mockingbird* emphasizes the ideas of honesty and standing up for your beliefs. And it shows that getting along with the majority is sometimes very wrong.

The book is filled with characters who display contrasting attitudes and morals. In fact, every major character seems to symbolize some philosophy of life, and each of them has a lesson to teach. Mrs. Dubose is an unpleasant old lady, going through morphine withdrawal, who believes that Atticus Finch is wrong in representing the black man on trial. She displays this attitude for Atticus's children by referring to their father with some of the most offensive racial slurs imaginable. But in the context of their use, her words are clearly a reflection on the speaker, not the person at whom they are directed. In contrast, Atticus responds to her with the same respect and consideration he gives everyone. He is disgusted with her actions, but he is not swayed. Atticus is just as disgusted and unswayed by Bob Ewell. Ewell is a piece of human vermin who has badly beaten his daughter and accused Tom Robinson of assaulting her. He feels that because Tom Robinson is black, he should have none of the legal protections guaranteed by the Constitution. In Ewell's eyes, Tom Robinson and Atticus Finch should be helpless in the face of his accusations.

Atticus Finch, of course, is a man ahead of his time and a model for his children and for the reader. When the children question his reasons for defending Tom, he replies, "If I didn't, I couldn't hold my head up in town. I couldn't represent this county in the legislature. I couldn't even tell you or Jem not to do something again." Jem and Scout, like a lot of students who read the book, are growing up in a puzzling world. After they have thought about the morals and beliefs of the people around them, they begin to see through the prejudice and fear and understand that people are all pretty much alike.

To Kill a Mockingbird, the story of one town's struggle with human rights, shows how people react when their cultural assumptions are threatened. It teaches some important lessons about judging people and about living by your own principles. Although there may be profane language involved, there are also plot, morals, and history. These are the real keys to literature.

DISCUSS

1. What is the thesis of Jenni's essay? How well is it stated?
2. How does Jenni deal with the fact that the book has objectionable language? Is her approach effective? What might have been involved in gathering this information?
3. How much detail does she supply about her student sample in the second paragraph? She did not tell exactly how many students she talked to and what the percentages were. Why not?
4. What point do the references to Mrs. Dubose and Bob Ewell make? Why do you suppose Jenni kept them in the same paragraph? Would you have developed each as a separate paragraph? Why?
5. What is the purpose of the paragraph about Atticus and his children?

ACT

Write an essay using the inductive process. You may choose one of the following topics, a variation of one of those topics, or an appropriate idea of your own.

To help prepare your information, use a worksheet that states your tentative hypothesis and a description of your sample. Be sure to give details about the size of your sample, how and why you chose that sample, and any other information that shows how you maintained control over the guidelines for inductive reasoning.

1. Today's advertising misleads people about how to maintain a healthy lifestyle.
2. College requirements have strengthened the high school's curriculum.
3. Participation in extracurricular activities promotes character.
4. High school students should be required to take at least one course in each department before graduation.
5. Parents should be allowed to help select the books taught in literature courses.

Refutation

Mark was waiting at the curb as Julie drove up to his house, and she could see he was upset even before he climbed into the car. Knowing her friend as well as she did, Julie knew she wouldn't have to ask what the problem was. And she was right. Mark had never been the type to hold anything in, and he was waving a newspaper clipping across the seat toward her.

"I can't get over the nerve of this guy. Who does he think he is? Did you see this column in last night's *Gazette,* Julie?"

"What are you talking about? You know I had to work last night. Of course I didn't see it." Julie let the clutch out and pulled away from the curb. "So tell me. What's it all about, anyway?"

"Well, it was on the editorial page. This guy wrote a guest opinion all about teenage alcohol problems and how he could solve everything in about two weeks. The man is insane. Naturally, my folks pointed it out."

"What's wrong with that? Like it or not, it's a problem and something should be done. Aren't your parents still involved in that Mothers Against Drunk Driving group? And, as far as that goes, you're never preaching to anybody, but I notice you don't drink either." Julie slowed for the corner and turned toward school.

"That's not the point. This guy doesn't know what he's talking about, and he goes on as if he were some kind of expert. For one thing, he's been retired for ten years. Do you suppose he even knows anybody our age?"

"How would I know? People have grandchildren."

"He claims that stricter laws will stop teenagers from drinking. Like kids are going to pay attention to the law when everybody else is doing what they want. Then he talks about how parents should be able to control their kids. He says that if parents had to spend the night in jail with their kids, there would be a lot less drinking. He thinks parents can know what their kids are doing every minute they're out of the house."

Julie laughed. "He does sound a little out of touch."

"No kidding. Then he said that kids drink because their parents don't watch them closely enough. I hate to bring up school, but didn't we study something about cause-and-effect statements that don't make sense? It really makes me mad that people take guys like this seriously."

Julie pulled into the left-turn lane and waited for a car to pass before she headed into the school's parking lot. "You are a little steamed. So what are you going to do about it? Write your own guest column? You'd look pretty good in print, you know."

"Any more writing like this, and I just might. Somebody ought to point out how ignorant this is."

Not every piece of writing that gets printed makes sense. Sometimes, especially when opinions are being expressed, you see factual errors and poor thinking that are impossible to ignore. Most of the time, you probably laugh or complain to your friends, and then forget about it. But every so often, you know enough about the topic to wish you could correct the errors and straighten out the writer's thinking.

Proving someone is wrong by offering a counter argument or additional information is called *refutation*. It has a unique purpose—correcting someone else's written arguments—and a unique method.

When you refute someone's mistaken ideas, you need to read that person's work very carefully to see exactly what caused the problem. In most writing the problem can be traced to one of three sources. The writer may be unqualified to write on the topic, may have used poor evidence, or may have made logical errors. Any one of these, or a combination of them, could make a writer's conclusion invalid. Your first step will be to examine the essay with each of these areas of weakness in mind.

Examine Background and Evidence

Background

Many people feel qualified to speak out on any topic that comes to their mind. Dozens of newspaper columnists make a good living doing just that, and the reading public seems to take them very seriously. Any opinions expressed by Mike Royko, Mary McGrory, or Ellen Goodman are going to be taken seriously. In fact, almost anything that appears in print will be taken seriously by a lot of people who seem to believe some mysterious gatekeeper would prevent publication if the information weren't 100 percent true. This attitude makes it all the more important that readers be alert to the possibility that some writers are not as qualified as they should be.

Almost every daily newspaper runs occasional guest columns in which readers are invited to express ideas on a topic more thoroughly than can be done in a letter to the editor. These columns are widely read, even when they express views a thoughtful person might strongly disagree with. Quite often the author has little qualification to write on the topic. Self-confidence seems to be the only criterion.

In the essay Mark was so upset about, the writer was old enough so that Mark might be justified in questioning whether he was well informed about the kinds of responsibilities, opportunities, and peer pressures involved in a teenager's decisions about alcohol. If it has been forty years since the writer was a teenager, he may be remembering a world that no longer exists. That is not to say that he couldn't be well informed but, since he didn't make his qualifications clear, the reader has no way of knowing. It is the writer's responsibility to foresee questions and deal with them.

The writer's relationship to the problem discussed is also worth investigating. Is there any reason to think that this person has experience with the teenage drinking problem? Even a sales clerk in a local convenience store that handles beer would be better informed than someone who knows only what he sees in the newspaper. If the writer has some experience that makes him knowledgeable, the reader has a right to know. And the writer has the responsibility to make it clear.

Of course, on another topic, a writer could be too young to have an understanding of the situation, or so involved in the problem that he or she cannot be objective. It's even possible that a person's location could affect opinion. For example, a person who lives next to a proposed interstate highway has concerns different from those of the factory owner whose transportation problems might be solved by the highway. A writer's opinion could be questioned for any of several reasons, and you must be aware of these personal elements. Don't expect anyone to be completely objective. That's not human nature. But do be aware of factors that might affect the writer's point of view.

Evidence

It's reasonable to demand that the writer's evidence be sound, and you have to judge that evidence on several bases.

On some topics, up-to-date information is absolutely necessary because the subject is constantly changing. For instance, an essay about privacy will be inaccurate without the latest information about national computer networks that can gain access to your financial, medical, and employment records. For other topics, the age of the evidence is irrelevant. If a writer is discussing the moral questions associated with euthanasia, he or she may not need the latest research.

Sometimes, because of your familiarity with the situation, you know a writer has used evidence that is not typical. Unrealistic or exaggerated examples prove little, and if an example is a one-of-a-kind situation, it should never be mentioned. The writer who tries to prove a business is crooked, for example, with an anecdote about a friend who felt he was cheated is not being fair. Exceptions do not prove the rule, especially when you don't know the circumstances.

At other times, you may not question the typicality of evidence, but you may have a real question about whether the writer has presented enough. There is no hard and fast rule about how much evidence is enough. It depends on the length of the paper and the complexity of the argument. A 500-word paper about television comedy may not require more than two or three good examples, but a paper on nuclear disarmament might have to be two or three times as long and have more fully developed examples to adequately support the thesis. Watch out for the writer who generalizes with insufficient evidence.

Finally, the writer's evidence must be relevant. You have seen and heard arguments in which the examples may have been interesting but did not illustrate the point the writer wanted to make. The writer who wants to convince you that Americans are not serious about fighting air pollution proves nothing with an example involving plastic trash bags or disposable diapers. Another writer who says computers are revolutionizing education is off the mark when raving about how children love to play computer games.

SUMMARY

Refutation points out the mistakes and poor thinking in someone else's writing. These flaws may stem from the writer's background and from the evidence used to support the thesis.

A writer's point of view may be affected by age, relationship to the problem, and even location. The evidence used to support the thesis may be questioned if it is not recent enough or is not representative. The writer may also have given too little evidence or have used irrelevant evidence.

DISCUSS

1. Why do so many people assume that, if something appears in print, it must be true?
2. How might a writer's background affect his or her credibility? Name two factors in a person's background that could affect that person's opinion.
3. On what kind of topic might up-to-date information be important? Give an example of a topic where the evidence may not have to be recent.
4. How can you tell when a writer has presented enough evidence to be convincing?

ACT

Look through a number of weekly newsmagazines, such as *Newsweek, Time,* and *U.S. News and World Report,* that contain opinion articles.

Find an essay with which you disagree. You don't need to disagree with everything the writer says, but the more differences you have, the better.

1. State the bibliographical information for the article. Include the title, author, magazine, and date published.
2. What is the thesis of the article? Quote it exactly. If it is only implied, quote the words that come closest to actually stating the thesis.
3. What opinion or opinions do you disagree with? List as many as you can. Quote each statement exactly. If the ideas are implied instead of stated directly, quote the words that imply the idea.
4. For each disagreement you find, explain in one or two sentences exactly why you feel as you do.

FOR YOUR JOURNAL

Some incidents are so common to human experience that they seem almost universal. Nearly everyone has experienced the frustration of having to get to an important appointment and being sabotaged at the last minute by a car that won't start.

Another almost universal human experience is the discussion in which you get so angry that you can't think straight and end up saying something pointless. You may be dealing with a rude salesclerk or trying to renew your driver's license, but the feeling is the same. Then, after the moment has passed and the person is gone, you spend minutes, maybe hours, rehashing the discussion and daydreaming about what you should have said.

It is always easier to come up with the appropriate reaction after the heat of the moment has passed, and it's natural to relieve the tension within yourself by going over and over "what I should have said."

When was the last time this happened to you? It might have been today or yesterday or a month ago, but you can probably remember it vividly. In your journal, write down the conversation as it should have happened. Take the time to cross out, rewrite, and make your comments as perfect as possible. Tell the person exactly how you feel. Make your position perfectly clear.

Examine the Logic

A fallacy is a breakdown of the reasoning process. The logic of a fallacious argument has some flaw, accidental or intentional, that makes the conclusion suspect. While fallacious reasoning should immediately make you suspicious, don't automatically assume that the conclusion is false. It may be possible to reach the same conclusion through another, more logical, line of reasoning. But your response must be the same. You need to examine the essay very closely to see if the conclusion will hold up. And that conclusion must be supported by some other evidence.

A complete list of fallacious arguments could make a book in itself. What's more, not all of the suspicious reasoning you see has a formal title, but an understanding of typical fallacies will help you spot everyday illogic in your reading. Familiarize yourself with these fallacies.

Appeal to Authority

The appeal to authority cites an expert, but outside of his or her field of knowledge.

Quoting an authority is a useful means of gaining support for a writer's opinion. If the writer can show that an expert agrees, readers will often be impressed and tend to think the author's ideas merit serious consideration. And it is logical to believe that your chances of being correct are better if you have experts on your side.

A problem arises, however, when the writer cites an authority who is widely admired, but in an unrelated field. For instance, a writer discussing motorcycle helmet laws might quote a famous actor on the topic. If a popular young actor says riders should be required to wear helmets, that opinion has a lot of influence on some people. But should it? What training does the actor have to make him an expert on helmet laws?

The actor very likely does not have an engineering degree. Probably, he does not have a medical degree either. Or extensive experience that allowed him to observe the difference between injuries suffered by those wearing and those not wearing helmets. Almost certainly, he is not a statistician who has carefully recorded and studied accident records and the types of injuries suffered. And it is just as likely that he has no legal background to make him an expert on constitutional law. No matter how well known, he is still a private citizen speaking strictly from his rather limited, personal experience.

As with most topics worth discussing, however, there is another side to this question. The fact that this person is a well-known actor and not an expert in any of the fields mentioned does not mean that he is incapable of forming an intelligent opinion. His opinion is probably about as good as that of any other nonexpert you could ask. He should not be dismissed as worthless because he is an actor, but neither should his opinion be given credibility it does not deserve.

Begging the Question

Begging the question is a fallacy that assumes what it is trying to prove.

In effect, the writer is saying that what is assumed to be true is true. Or, the blue sky is blue. In practice, of course, begging the question is not nearly so ridiculous sounding and can be difficult to detect.

When you were a child, you may have experienced the frustration of being asked to explain when you had no ready explanation.

"Why are you fighting with Terri?"

"Because!"

"Why?"

"Just because. That's all."

Begging the question is little more than an adult version of the same circular conversation. "Women should not be allowed to join male-only clubs because the clubs are not intended for women" totally ignores the real question that begs to be answered— "Why should some clubs be reserved exclusively for male membership?"

The administration of one high school decided to raise the standards for students who could register for Advanced Placement English classes. The students had to have at least a B average in English. This angered some students who felt they were as talented as students with higher grades—they had simply chosen to not work as hard. One senior was so angry that he wrote a letter to the school newspaper saying, "Refusing to admit students who are qualified for the Advanced Placement courses is unfair."

Whether the students are qualified is, of course, the question the administration hoped to answer by looking at their grades. It is possible that other criteria could be used, but simply saying that students who have low grades are just as qualified as anyone else does not make them so. The letter writer assumed what he tried to demonstrate.

False Cause

The Latin term for this fallacy is *Post hoc, ergo propter hoc.* "After this, therefore because of this." The writer of a false-cause argument claims that because one event came before another, the first event caused the second. While it is possible that the first event did cause the second, the time relationship alone is not sufficient evidence.

For years people have argued about the effects of capital punishment. Some support their opinions by pointing to countries that have outlawed capital punishment and experienced a decrease in the murder rate. Others point to countries that did the same thing and saw an increase in the murder rate. What both sides overlook is that there were undoubtedly other changes taking place at the same time the laws were amended. None of the countries that outlawed capital punishment did so in a vacuum. Police methods continue to develop, procedures for reporting crimes change, and economic conditions rise and fall constantly. A change in the law is not the only influence on murder rates.

The fact that one event followed another might be meaningful, but it just as easily might not. To establish the cause-effect relationship, the writer needs to provide additional evidence.

Faulty Analogy

An analogy is often useful in explaining an idea because it compares the unfamiliar to the familiar. But the analogy does not give proof of anything. Analogies can only be perfect if the two things discussed are identical, and that is unlikely. In that sense, all analogies are faulty.

Strict school-attendance policies are almost always unpopular. When students ask why they are required to be in every class every day, the answer is often, "It's just like your parents having to be at their place of work. They have to show up for work every day, and you have to go to school every day. They can't decide to skip an hour of work and neither can you."

The analogy, like most, makes a point but is far from perfect. The reasons behind the school's policy and the company's policy are different. Students are required to be present so that they can learn, something that is to their own advantage. Employees are required to be present for the company's benefit, so the paperwork can be completed, the product manufactured, or the packages delivered.

The personal consequences of absence are also different. The student might have to make up time; the employee will lose wages and may eventually lose the job. While there are many similarities between school and the workplace, there are also many differences, and these make the analogy a poor argument. Certainly, many good reasons can be given to justify attendance at school, but the parental-employment analogy is not convincing.

Appeal to Ignorance

The writer who uses the appeal to ignorance claims that something must be true because no one has been able to prove it false, or that something is false because no one has proven it true. This argument shifts the burden of proof from the person making the claim to the reader. Medical frauds used to claim that copper bracelets would cure arthritis because no one had been able to prove they wouldn't.

When a suburban hospital bought an apartment house to be used as a hospice for dying AIDS patients, several people in the neighborhood objected. The city council called a special meeting to inform people about how the house was to be used and to give the neighbors a chance to voice their concerns. After the basic information about when the house would be occupied and who would live there was explained, one man questioned whether present zoning restrictions allowed such a use. Some said yes, some said no, and the city attorney said the matter was not clear because no one had considered the possibility of residential health-care facilities when the zoning laws were written. After a two-hour meeting, nothing had been settled to anyone's satisfaction, and council members decided to study the matter further.

In the next day's newspaper, an editorial blasted the hospice proposal. The editorial mentioned several objections, but one point received special emphasis. "While we do not deny that such housing is a good idea, there seems to be no reason why it must be in a residential neighborhood. No one has ever offered a shred of proof that property values will not plummet as soon as the hospice's presence becomes known."

Probably true. No one has proven that property values won't go down. How could anyone prove that? Remember, it is very possible that property values might change. No one said they wouldn't. The point is that property values have not been discussed, and the burden of proof is on the people who make the claim. If they can offer some evidence that values will drop, they may have a legitimate complaint, but it is their job to find the evidence. They could as easily claim that no one has proved the hospice won't cause cancer and demand proof that it won't.

Argument to the Person

An argument to the person shifts the discussion from ideas to an attack on the person who represents the other side. The writer either diverts attention from the issues or transfers negative feelings about the person to the issues being discussed.

In politics, campaigns often seem to degenerate into personal attacks on the opposing candidate. Assuming that the real issue should be the manner in which your city, state, or country will be governed for the next few years, details about a candidate's social or family life are usually irrelevant. In recent history candidates have been the target of attacks because they were divorced, humorless, black, career soldiers, actors, Catholic, homosexual, farmers, Jewish, intellectual, wimpy, too ethnic, too rich, too clumsy, or too privileged. Whether the labels are accurate or not, voters should, of course, concentrate on how the candidates perform in their jobs.

Remember, however, that accusations may be relevant if they involve the job performance or character of the person. Dishonesty and poor judgment in the past may indicate that you could expect dishonesty and poor judgment in the future.

Argument to Pity

The person who uses this argument plays on your sympathy by bringing up facts that are irrelevant to the issue. Bob, a high school junior, tried this approach as the end of the semester neared.

"Mr. Dennis, I know I haven't been doing well this semester. Could you tell me what grade you're going to give me?"

"Until semester tests are completed, I won't know for sure what grade you've earned, Bob. But right now you only have a C average. And it's low enough so that you shouldn't expect the semester test to make a massive difference. What happened to your semester project anyway? When we talked a week ago, you said it was almost done."

"Well, I've been having some personal problems. I can't talk about them, but I hope you can give me the benefit of the doubt. I really need a B."

"How could I do that, Bob? We've talked about this before. Nobody gives you grades; you have to earn them."

"Mr. Dennis, this is really hard to ask, but my family has been planning to send me to France next year, and if I don't have at least a B average, I can't go. Couldn't you see your way clear to raise the grade, just a little?"

This conversation could go on for a long time because Bob seems to catch on slowly and Mr. Dennis may yet weaken, but the ploy is obvious, and so is the faulty logic. Bob's personal problems and the trip to France are irrelevant to the question of what grade he has earned.

Argument to Popular Attitudes

This fallacy plays on people's emotional reactions to commonly popular or unpopular ideas. Concepts like love of country, racial or religious fears, and admiration for traditional values all produce predictable reactions from people.

Since the reactions you can expect vary from one group to another, the argument will often be written for a specific audience. Young people will not always react in the same way as older people. East coast residents may react one way, West coast residents another. City dwellers may not see things the same way as rural people.

Some attitudes, however, are almost universal. The car dealer who tapes his television ad surrounded by his beautiful wife and three adorable children is almost certain to improve his credibility. People react positively to the traditional values of home and family. The advertisement isn't likely to offer any evidence about the worth of his cars, but it will leave the desired impression. Here is a man to be admired. Like all good Americans, he takes his family obligations seriously.

Former President Richard Nixon used this technique in his famous Checkers speech. He had been accused of misappropriating $18,000 in campaign funds during his 1952 campaign for the vice-presidency. Nixon went on radio and television to explain his use of the money.

About half way through the speech, then-Senator Nixon detailed his personal financial worth and, after making the point that he was not a rich man, he said of his wife, "Pat doesn't have a mink coat. But she does have a respectable Republican cloth coat. And I always tell her that she'd look good in anything.

"One other thing I probably should tell you because, if I don't, they'll probably be saying this about me too. We did get something—a gift—after the election. A man down in Texas heard Pat on the radio mention the fact that our two youngsters would like to have a dog. And, believe it or not, the day before we left on this campaign trip, we got a message from Union Station in Baltimore saying they had a package for us. We went down to get it. You know what it was.

"It was a little cocker spaniel dog in a crate that he sent all the way from Texas. Black-and-white spotted. And our little girl—Trisha, the 6-year old—named it Checkers. And you know, the kids love the dog and I just want to say this right now, that regardless of what they say about it, we're gonna keep it."

In just a few paragraphs, Richard Nixon managed to appeal to popular attitudes by showing that he was not well off, that he loved and admired his wife, that he was concerned about his daughters, and loved puppies.

Red Herring

For years stories have been told about tracking escaped convicts with bloodhounds. According to the stories, the dogs could be thrown off the scent by dragging the carcass of a dead animal across the trail. Apparently red herrings are especially smelly because this fallacy refers to any attempt at introducing a new topic with the intention of diverting a reader from the important issue.

Officials of one national fund-raising organization were accused of stealing millions of dollars in contributions intended for cancer research. Newspaper, magazine, and television advertisements sponsored by the organization had talked about how close a cure was, if only more money were available. But investigators found that less than 15 percent of the money ended up in the hands of researchers. About 25 percent was used for advertising and expenses. The remaining 60 percent was used for lining officials' pockets. Most medical charities are legitimate, but this one gave them all a black eye.

Naturally, as soon as the accusations were made public, contributions went down. The officials were ready for that. The president of the organization held a press conference at which he said, "We must not allow misunderstandings, organizational problems, or legal matters that are yet to be settled to get in the way of our fight against cancer. Patients still need to be treated with the latest, most humane techniques possible.

"Toward that end, we will be establishing a series of cancer treatment centers in ten major cities across the United States. Since these centers of excellence will be available to all, regardless of ability to pay, we are instituting a new goal for this year. By the end of the year, we want to have a 35 million dollar emergency fund to finance our expanded war on cancer."

None of the legal and financial difficulties have been explained, but he has introduced a new project intended to shift attention from the probability that a lot of money will never reach the people it was intended for. And many contributors will fall for it.

You Also

This is a variation of the argument to the person. The writer tries to show that the stand someone has taken on an issue is insincere and hypocritical. It happened only a few years ago in an Iowa governor's race.

The campaign had been quiet, with the voters showing little interest. The issues were standard ones that seem to come up at every election: tax reform, school funding, law and order. None of them really excited the voters.

Since it was a major plank in her party's platform, one candidate had been speaking regularly on the need to make tax laws more fair. She insisted that loopholes allowed many people with high incomes to pay no taxes. She was attracting attention with the argument; voters always agree that the rich should pay their fair share of taxes. Polls had her leading by a good margin when the bottom fell out of her campaign.

As it turned out, she did know all about loopholes. A reporter for a major daily newspaper discovered that she made use of some loopholes herself. In the previous year, she had income of approximately $100,000 and paid no tax. She was not guilty of tax evasion; what she had done was legal. Most of her income was from nontaxable sources, none from wages, and she had simply taken advantage of the deductions and exclusions that the state law allowed.

Voters didn't care about the question of legality. Saying that everyone should pay taxes and, at the same time, paying no taxes herself made the candidate look like a hypocrite.

Remember, she did not say that people should pay more tax than they legally owed. She wanted the tax law changed, and the change would have done away with her own deductions. No matter. Attention had been diverted from the question of tax reform to the question of whether one of the candidates was living up to the spirit of her argument.

SUMMARY

Fallacies can occur in anyone's writing. Whether accidental or intentional, they always call into question the writer's conclusion. Some fallacies change the subject, others misdirect by more imaginative means, but all can be convincing if the reader is not alert.

Ten of the most common fallacies are begging the question, false cause, faulty analogy, red herring, you also, and arguments to authority, ignorance, person, pity, and popular attitudes.

DISCUSS

1. What do all fallacies have in common?
2. Explain how an argument could be fallacious and still have a valid conclusion. How can you determine if the conclusion is valid?
3. At least half of the fallacies you've studied divert attention from the issue being discussed. Identify three fallacies that divert attention, and give an example of each.
4. One dictionary defines the word capricious as "having a tendency toward caprice." It uses the word being defined in the definition. How does begging the question resemble the process of defining a word by using the word itself?
5. In what way is it accurate to say that all analogies are faulty?

ACT

Name and explain the fallacy in each of the following statements.

1. Anyone who has ever worn a helmet while riding a motorcycle knows that peripheral vision is decreased, hearing is distorted, extreme heat causes fatigue, and additional wind resistance strains the rider's neck. As a result, helmets are unsafe.

2. Most juvenile crime takes place between the hours of 10:00 *p.m.* and 2:00 *a.m.* What this town needs is a curfew to get the kids off the streets.

3. Most crack addicts started by using marijuana. Those who want to decriminalize marijuana are playing into the hands of cocaine dealers.

4. No one has yet proved conclusively that smoking causes cancer.

5. I just don't feel comfortable with Dr. Geronoski's advice about losing weight. The man must be fifty pounds overweight himself, you know.

6. It's a well-known fact that our police are totally ineffective.

7. When I was a boy, my father insisted that I stand up to the neighborhood bully. America can't afford to let itself be pushed around by global bullies.

8. Exxon is already spending millions of dollars on cleanup operations. In these hard times, it's unreasonable to expect more of them.

9. College athletics are serious business and have nothing to do with academics. It's time we stop being hypocritical. College is a farm club for professional sports, and we should be paying the athletes.

10. Beverly Cleary's filthy books should be banned from the library.

11. Senator Clark's ideas for a national health plan are nothing but rehashed socialism.

12. The union cannot afford to give in to management. Think of the struggles former members went through to win benefits over the years.

13. Marcy is pretty serious about astrology, and you certainly can't prove it isn't true. I guess she's got a point.

14. *Nutrition for Athletes* must be a pretty good book. After all, it was written by an athlete.

15. Jim's parents are always complaining about the availability of drugs in town, but they think nothing of tossing off a couple of martinis while watching television.

FOR YOUR JOURNAL

Sophists were ancient Greek teachers who earned a bad reputation by practicing all the arts of deceit. Intentional fallacies were their specialty. In a courtroom, Sophists were great, but not if you were concerned about justice. Their stature was lowered even further by the fact that, for a fee, they would teach anyone their methods of argument.

Today, the meaning of the word has changed very little. A modern sophist is a person who uses psychologically appealing techniques to mislead readers or listeners. A sophistical argument is one that is deliberately misleading.

A knowledge of sophistry is, of course, a double-edged sword. The person who recognizes misleading arguments is perfectly capable of using them on someone else. And the person who can use them on someone else is probably best equipped to recognize and defend against them. Of course, writers should not deliberately use fallacies in a real discussion, but there is a lot to be gained by experimenting with them.

As an exercise in making yourself more knowledgeable about misleading arguments, use your journal to write several fallacious arguments.

Assume that you are trying to return some article to a department store. The purchase was made two months ago, and you have used and abused the article you are returning. It is now in poor condition, and the clerk knows it should not be returned. Write three different arguments and use a different fallacy in each. Remember, your purpose is not to lie but to use fallacies that might be convincing. Identify the fallacies you are using.

Structure Your Refutation

The framework of your refutation is similar to the one you used in other essays. It has a beginning, a middle, and an end. But the circumstances of refutation require differences in strategy.

In most other essays, you can assume the audience is in a more or less receptive frame of mind. Many of them read your work because they are interested in the topic and want to learn more about it. At the least, your audience is somewhat friendly. With refutation, you must assume that the people you most need to reach—those who have been taken in by the other person's misleading arguments—disagree with you from the outset.

This is a narrow audience. You will not be likely to reach many of the people who completely agreed with the other writer. Their minds were made up long ago, and they probably hold the same erroneous notions. And there is nothing to be gained by telling them off. Your best reason for writing a refutation is to reach those who either have been convinced by the writer or are swaying in that direction. They are an audience that will be easily offended if you start out with a direct personal attack.

Introduction

The purpose of your introduction is to bring up the topic in a natural manner. In this case, it may be sufficient to identify the essay you are concerned about. Tell where you saw it, the title, the author, and the general topic. The difference comes with the thesis sentence. The usual thesis sentence simply states the point you want to make:

"Caroline Smith makes several errors of judgment when she claims that Clinton needs a new east-west freeway."

But the refutation thesis sentence can take on an added function. It presents an opportunity for you to establish yourself as a reasonable person who tries to see both sides of an argument. You want the audience to see you in the most receptive light possible. With that in mind, write your thesis sentence in two parts: a concession statement and an assertion statement.

"Although Caroline Smith's desire for a thriving business community is one we should all share, she makes several errors of judgment when she claims that Clinton needs a new east-west freeway."

Notice that the concession part of the thesis doesn't give her much. It simply acknowledges that her intentions are good, not that you agree with what she proposes.

Body

Plan the body of your refutation exactly as you would for any other essay. You have several points you want to make about the author's argument. Each of those differences of opinion will be one of your subpoints and, therefore, a paragraph.

Decide ahead of time what will be the most effective order to deal with them. Structure each of those paragraphs around a strong topic sentence and use the familiar methods of paragraph development.

If your topic sentence refers to something the writer said, it is a good idea to quote the statement you are disagreeing with. If the quote would take too much space, you can paraphrase. You do not want to be accused of misquoting, so be careful to paraphrase accurately. When possible, make a concession to each quote. If that is impossible, at least remember to be mannerly.

Then, explain exactly what is wrong with the statement you are objecting to. If your objection is not to something the author said but to his or her methods, say so. If the writer has used a misleading example, give several better examples that will make your point. If the writer has misinterpreted examples, show clearly, simply, and rationally what is wrong with the examples given. If the writer used fallacious reasoning, explain the fallacy as well as possible.

Conclusion

You can use any of the methods of conclusion studied in Chapter 2. Again, it is a good idea to make a concession to the writer. However you choose to close your refutation, remember to be mannerly and not fall into name calling.

The following essay was written to show Joseph Kelly's objections to an opinion column that had been printed in his local newspaper. Read the essay and answer the questions that follow it.

Joseph Kelly
Composition II
Mr. Lewis
April 7, 19____

Control the Guns

On March 13, the opinion page of the *Tribune* featured an essay by Mr. Byron Williams. Mr. Williams argued against stricter controls on hand-gun sales in Iowa and across the nation. He has a right to his opinion, but if there is any danger of readers being misled, they should be aware of several problems. Mr. Williams's essay, while I'm sure it was well intentioned, was flawed by his own narrow point of view, atypical quotes, and several instances of fallacious reasoning.

Mr. Williams is not a disinterested party who can be expected to have a balanced view of the situation. According to his own statement, he is a collector who owns several dozen handguns that he has acquired over the years. He derives a great deal of enjoyment from possessing and using these guns. Probably, there is no harm in that, but it is certain that Mr. Williams could not be expected to mention any of the statistics showing the relationship of legally owned handguns to suicides, accidents resulting in death, and impulsive violence. If Mr. Williams doesn't mention these facts because he is not aware of them, he is no authority. If he ignores them because he thinks they are silly or inaccurate, he is letting his hobby govern his opinions.

Mr. Williams also quotes several people whose opinions could have been predicted if he had identified them fully. The quotes are predictable in that they seem to rehash very old National Rifle Association (NRA) arguments. For instance, he quotes Joe Foss, "The way the justice system is working these days, we need more arms." It would have been helpful if he had mentioned that Mr. Foss is a former president of the NRA. That was followed by a quote from J. Warren Cassidy referring to "anti-gunners and anti-hunters who want to take away your Second Amendment right to own and use firearms, and end hunting too." Mr. Cassidy is the current executive vice president of the NRA. While both men are involved in the gun-control debate, neither of them is without an ax to grind.

Mr. Williams's third authority is even less appropriate. Two paragraphs were used to detail Arthur Taylor's military background and combat experience. Mr. Taylor served his nation well in two wars, and we should respect him for that, but being a war hero does not make a man an expert on the need for handguns in civilian life.

The use of an inappropriate authority was not the only fallacy contained in the essay. Mr. Williams later quoted Arthur Taylor as saying that he wanted to be able to protect his family. Mr. Williams later said he wanted his daughter to be able to "defend herself if need be." No one wants to see either man's family left helpless, but both of these appeals to pity are irrelevant. The question is whether the sale of handguns should be more strictly controlled. No one has proposed taking away the guns owned by these two citizens.

In the heated arguments over what to do about the ease with which criminals arm themselves, a lot of people say things that deserve a second look. Some of them should be looked at closely because they are reasonable arguments that deserve consideration. Others need inspection for entirely different reasons. They may at first seem logical, but they really don't make much sense when you think about them.

DISCUSS

1. How is the audience of a refutation essay unique? Explain fully.
2. What is the thesis of Joseph Kelly's essay? How is it different from most theses? What is the purpose of this difference?
3. What are Joseph Kelly's supporting points for this thesis? Are they clear enough? If not, how could they be improved?
4. Analyze paragraphs two and three. If they are well developed, what development do you see? If they need more explanation, what would you suggest?
5. How good are the introduction and conclusion? Explain.

ACT

Write a refutation essay in which you respond to some writer whose ideas you disagree with. You may use the article you outlined earlier in this chapter, or you may find a new one. Remember that you do not need to disagree with everything the writer said.

If you cannot locate an essay with which you completely, or almost completely, disagree, use several essays on the same subject. In this case, your paper will respond to several opinions with which you disagree, but those opinions could be found in separate essays written about the same subject. If Joseph Kelly had aimed his refutation at several essays, he might have used this thesis statement: "While most of the people writing against more restrictive gun laws are well intentioned, each of them seems to have at least one serious flaw in his or her opinion."

The Research Paper

Focusing on a Subject

Choosing an appropriate subject for your research paper can be challenging. You'll be living with the choice for several weeks, and that fact alone makes it an important step. More significant, though, is the fact that a research paper offers you a rare opportunity to determine what you are going to study in school. You may, within limits, decide what courses to take, but almost invariably the content of those courses is beyond your control. With the research paper, however, you have permission to get excited about and dig into a subject that matters to *you*.

There is a dark side to everything, of course. If you tend to avoid decisions, you'll have to change your methods. Also, be certain that you understand the assignment fully. Listen carefully as the teacher explains the type of paper you are to write, how long it should be, and any limits on your choice of subject. If the subject is assigned, or limited, a large part of your decision has been made. More commonly, though, you are on your own.

When you know a research opportunity is coming up, look for interesting possibilities in newspapers or magazines, or in your journal entries. If you are taking a particularly interesting course this semester, ask the teacher for some ideas about related topics. The teacher will be flattered, and you might discover a really great idea. Remember, the possibilities are limitless, but you need to come up with something important enough to excite you. And you need to move quickly.

You also need to move with reasonable certainty that the topic will work for you. A mistake at this point could force you into the position of searching for information that either isn't very abundant or, worse yet, you don't really care about. Don't put off thinking about your choice of topic until just before you start the actual research. Leave enough time to choose a topic you care about and can handle in the time and space you have available.

As you consider the possibilities, keep these guidelines in mind.

1. Do you really care about the subject?
2. Will enough information be available?
3. Can you complete the research in the time available?
4. Can the subject be covered in the pages allowed?
5. Is the subject important enough to justify taking your time?

If you make the right decisions now, the research project can give you two things: a reason to get excited about an idea, and the time to do something about it.

Write a Tentative Outline

Immediately after you choose a topic, even before you set foot in the library, write a preliminary outline. This may seem premature, but it is very important that you give your research some direction as soon as possible. Writing the preliminary outline forces you to make some decisions about what it is that you really want to learn. Don't be concerned about details—just jot down some questions that you would like to see answered. What do you want to learn in this research project? Here's an outline that one student, Don Schmidt, wrote after deciding that he'd like to find out more about the Berlin Wall. Notice that he didn't bother with an introduction or a conclusion at this time, and that the outline is in the form of questions to be answered.

Introduction—Save for later.
  I. What, specifically, prompted erection of the wall?
 II. Who first came up with the idea?
III. How did people react at the time?
IV. What effects did the wall have on families?
 V. How did it affect those who crossed the border to work?
VI. How did people get necessities that came from outside?
Conclusion—Save for later.

When you begin looking for information about your topic, the outline should help you to distinguish between what is useful and what is not. It also forces you to be sure you know what your topic actually is, and it helps to determine the purpose of your paper. The preceding outline seems to have narrowed the topic to "What are some of the original reasons for and effects of the Berlin Wall?" Don noticed right away that he had two separate topics. Under some circumstances, that might have been acceptable, but since his research paper was going to be only ten to twelve pages long, he decided to ignore the causes behind the wall and concentrate on the effects it had on people living near it.

SUMMARY

Choosing an interesting subject for your research paper is one of the most important steps in the whole project. Once you are certain that you understand the assignment, look for possibilities until you find an idea that excites you. Start early enough to find the perfect subject.

Immediately after you choose a topic, even before going to the library, write a preliminary outline. Don't be concerned about details. Simply jot down some questions that you would like to see answered. The outline should provide guidance when you start looking for information about your topic. It also forces you to put into words exactly what you are looking for.

DISCUSS

1. Name and explain two reasons why selecting a topic is one of the most important steps in the research process.
2. The text described four sources of research topics. What would be another original place where you could get some ideas?
3. Describe the form of a preliminary outline.
4. What is the purpose of the preliminary outline?
5. How could a preliminary outline help narrow a topic that is too broad?

ACT

Carefully select a topic for your research paper. Your teacher will set a date when you must have the topic ready and a tentative outline prepared.

Gathering Resources

Descriptors

When you go to the library to look for information on your topic, your first inclination might be to race to the card catalog, look up your topic, and pull a few books from the shelves. That's not a bad idea, but, if you did it that way, you would probably miss a lot. Very likely, information on your topic can be found under not one but several headings. It's possible, in fact, that you could find much more information under a synonym for the word you have chosen, or under a term that is slightly different from but closely related to your topic.

First, brainstorm all the headings, or descriptors, you can think of that might relate to your topic. For instance, if you are researching the death penalty, you would undoubtedly find one or two sources under *death penalty,* but you would find a lot more if you also looked under *capital punishment, murder,* and possibly even *capital offense,* or *treason. Execution* and *electrocution* are other possibilities. Make a list of descriptors—words and names under which information is stored—that might apply to your topic.

Research Checklist

Next, make a research checklist. You will probably obtain information from several sources in the library. There are so many possibilities, in fact, that it is a good idea to start your investigation with a list of all those sources. You can start your checklist from the suggestions below, and your teacher or librarian may have some additional suggestions.

- Card Catalog. Look in the card catalog and write down the titles that look as if they might be useful. Don't check them out yet. You are making a tentative list of sources, and this step should occupy only a few minutes of your time. Be sure to look under each of your descriptors.
- *Readers' Guide to Periodical Literature.* Look in the last three or four annual volumes to get an idea of how much

information is available. This should tell you quickly if the topic is a good one or not. Record names of articles that look like they might be useful. Again, remember to look under each of your descriptors.

- Pamphlet File.
  If your school library has a pamphlet, or vertical, file, check to see if it contains information you can use.
- Special Encyclopedias. Most special encyclopedias will be kept in a central location. The *Encyclopedia of Bioethics, Encyclopedia of Crime and Justice,* and *Encyclopedia of the Social Sciences* are good examples. Your librarian will be able to direct you to others that might be helpful with your topic.

Depending on the resources available in your library, you may have even more sources of information to consult. List them all, and after each include any promising titles you find.

On-line Searching

Many school libraries now have the equipment needed to conduct computerized on-line searches. The most common and generally useful database is *Magazine Index,* which gives complete bibliographic information for nearly five hundred popular magazines. This information is updated daily, so the most recent articles are included.

If your library uses on-line searching, you will probably be given instructions on how to use the equipment. In some schools, one faculty member is in charge of all on-line searches and conducts the actual search after conferring with the student. In other schools, the student may conduct the search after some instruction. Whichever method is used, you will want to use the descriptors that have been most productive so far.

On-line searching is expensive, so you will probably discuss a search strategy with the librarian before actually going on-line. By determining beforehand what data base will be most useful for your topic, and what descriptors are most likely to yield the best results, you can find a wealth of information in a relatively short time. Usually, you will get a printout listing the sources found in the on-line search. The printout will include all bibliographic information needed to find the articles.

Compact Disc

You may be able to find the information you need by using a compact disc reader. Bibliographic information can be stored on the same type of compact disc that is used to record music. This technology allows massive amounts of information to be held on one disc, so the same information contained in several volumes of the *Readers' Guide* is now available in a small, easy to use format. Since the disc is updated monthly, you can find the most recent articles.

Once you have gathered a sizable list of possible sources, it is time to look for the actual printed material. If most of your material is in books, check them out. But the most useful information these days is usually found in periodicals—magazines and newspapers. Since they are generally published daily, weekly, or monthly, the information is much more likely to be current. If you can possibly do so, it will be to your advantage to concentrate on periodicals.

Because of electronically assisted research, you may find an article that looks interesting but is not available because your library doesn't subscribe to that periodical. Few libraries could afford to make them all available. Ask if the one you need can be obtained through a library sharing plan. FAX machines have made possible the sharing of printed material that would otherwise be unavailable. If you have enough time, photocopies can be mailed from one library to another.

If your library has a photocopy machine for student use, it is a good idea to make your own copy of the magazine articles you consult. Some libraries actually prefer that you make a copy rather than tie up the original. That way, the article is available for other students to use. From your point of view, it is more convenient to have a copy that you can underline or highlight as needed.

Working Bibliography

As a final step before beginning to take notes, you will need to create a working bibliography. You started one when you listed possible sources of information. This step just formalizes the procedure a little.

Your teacher will probably want you to use index cards for the working bibliography. Index cards offer many advantages, not the least of which is that you can rearrange them in any order you wish. For instance, you will begin with them in the order in which you first discover each source. Toward the end of your work, you may need to rearrange them for footnotes or endnotes. Then you will put them in alphabetical order when typing your list of works cited. At other times in the research and writing process, you may want to arrange them in order of importance, or usefulness, or any other order that suits your needs at the time. Index cards make the most flexible system of recording your working bibliography.

The bibliography card for a *book* or *pamphlet* should include:

1. Author's full name (last name first)
2. Full title (underlined, and including subtitle)
3. City of publication
4. Publisher
5. Year published

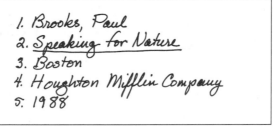

1. Brooks, Paul
2. Speaking for Nature
3. Boston
4. Houghton Mifflin Company
5. 1988

The bibliography card for a *magazine* or *newspaper* should include:

1. Author's full name (last name first)
2. Full title of article (in quotes)
3. Full title of periodical (underlined)
4. Date of publication
5. Page numbers (first and last)

1. Ross, Philip E.
2. "Clean Air Fuels for the 90's"
3. *Popular Science*
4. January 1990
5. 47-51

Record this information for each of the books or periodicals you plan to use. Then, as you discover new sources, you will need only a few minutes to add them to your collection. When the time comes to document your sources, the information will be immediately available.

There will always be a temptation to try what looks like an easier way, that is, to write all this information in a spiral notebook or not record it at all. It is not an easy way out. Taking one minute to record the information for each source on an index card will pay you back many times over.

This is also a good time to review your tentative outline. Your plans could need adjustment if you have been unable to find some information you were counting on. On the other hand, you may have discovered some new idea that hadn't occurred to you before looking for your sources.

SUMMARY

Begin your research by brainstorming all the descriptors that might lead to information on your topic. Then, make a research checklist to get an overview of how much material is available. List all the promising titles you find. If your library has facilities for an on-line search or has a compact disc reader, use those to find the most current material. Finally, put your working bibliography on index cards and update your tentative outline.

DISCUSS

1. Why is it important to make yourself aware of all possible descriptors for your topic?
2. What is a research checklist?
3. How would on-line searching and compact disc technology give you more recent information?
4. What is a working bibliography? Why is it advantageous to use index cards instead of a spiral notebook?
5. Describe the content of a bibliography card used for a book. How does it differ from the bibliography card for a magazine?

ACT
!!

It's time to begin your research. Review the preceding Summary, and go through the steps involved in gathering the material you need to read.

Reading and Taking Notes

Clear, concise, accurate notes will save you an enormous amount of time when you get to the writing part of your research project. Thorough and complete notes don't take much longer than careless ones, and you can work directly from those notes for your first draft. Thorough notes will also mean that you never have to go back to reread or verify material that you have already covered.

Take notes on index cards, the same size cards that you used for your bibliography. Using cards for your notes is even more advantageous than using them for your bibliography. You can sort your note cards according to author, subtopic, or source. You can put them in chronological order, or in the sequence in which you plan to use them. You can also reshuffle them quickly when you want to switch to another arrangement. When you compose your final paper, you can spread the note cards out on the floor or a large table and experiment with different organizational patterns. When it's time to document your sources, all the necessary information will be available in the correct order.

If at some time you need to add information, you can file new cards with the old without having to rewrite the whole collection. Furthermore, if you decide that some cards will not be as useful as you thought earlier, it is easy to dispose of them. Although you could store all your notes in a spiral notebook, you would be constantly tearing out, adding, and recopying. The flexibility of the card system will save you a lot of time and energy.

You should include four items of information on every note card.

1. Meaningful heading
2. Author's last name
3. Page numbers
4. Note

Meaningful Heading

Put the heading in the upper left-hand corner of the card. It will be useful in at least two ways. For instance, headings you use here could correspond to the major headings in your outline. The headings will then help you organize information as it goes into the first draft. Also, headings will help you locate those cards you need during the research process.

Author's Last Name

The author's name establishes a connection with your bibliography cards and, when you document sources, all the necessary information will be on the corresponding bibliography card. If a magazine article names no author, use the title. Whether you use author or title, it should match the first entry on the corresponding bibliography card.

Page Number

The exact page number will be necessary when you document sources. It is the one piece of information that is not included on the bibliography cards.

Note

There are three kinds of notes. You may summarize, paraphrase, or quote directly. The summary is useful if you want to include a lot of general information in a small space. A paraphrase will give you a more detailed record in your own words.

Three situations call for direct quotes. Use a direct quote if the original would be shorter than a paraphrase, if paraphrasing would take all the color out of the message, or if a paraphrase might not be as accurate. If there is any chance at all that you might need to use the writer's exact words, quote the material word for word, and use quotation marks carefully. Whenever you are in doubt, quote.

If you have your own photocopy of the text, consider cutting the quote you need from the article and gluing or taping it to the index card. Naturally, this is not possible if you are working from the original copy, but it does insure the accuracy of any quotes you use.

Be sure to record only one note on each card. If there is any possibility that the information you are saving will be used in different parts of your paper, use two note cards. If you put too much on one card, you will have an impossible task when you begin to group the cards according to the sequence in which they will be used. The only solution will be to rewrite the note, dividing the information between two cards.

Your note card should look like this.

Heading

Note _____

_____

_____

Author's name
Page number

The note-taking stage is also the best time to ensure against any accidental plagiarism. Most of the time, you hear the word *plagiarism* connected with wholesale theft of books, essays, or even ideas. In your situation, however, unintentional plagiarism is much more likely. You know that you cannot copy someone else's work, but you can fall into plagiarism in other ways, too. For instance, if your source has used a particularly original or catchy phrase, you must not use it yourself without using quotation marks and crediting the source. And, although you may use other people's ideas in your paper, you must always give them credit.

When your writing is completed, you will need to give credit to your sources in each of the following situations. First, you must give credit for all direct quotes. Second, give credit any time you use, in paraphrase or summary, information that is not common knowledge. Common knowledge is defined as information that is "common" to many sources. If you find the same information in three or four different articles, you can assume that it is well known and does not need to be documented. Finally, give credit any time you are in doubt. It is better to over-document than to be accused of stealing someone else's work. If you begin by recording your notes on index cards with all the necessary information, giving credit where credit is due will be automatic.

SUMMARY

Take notes on index cards. On each card include a heading, the author's last name, the exact page number, and the note itself. Copy the material word for word if there is any chance you might quote it in your paper. If there is no possibility of using it as a quote, you may paraphrase or summarize.

DISCUSS

1. List three reasons why index cards are preferable to a spiral notebook or to loose-leaf paper for taking notes.
2. Name the three pieces of information that must be included on the note card in addition to the note itself. What is the reason for including each of them?
3. List the three kinds of notes and give an example of a situation when each might be appropriate.

ACT

Begin taking notes for your research paper. Use index cards and be sure to include every piece of information that might be of use. If there is any doubt, make a note card. If you don't make the card and later need the information, it may be unavailable or very difficult to relocate. It is easier to throw the card out if you decide later not to use it.

Writing the First Draft

By this time, you probably have forty or fifty note cards. Each note card has a heading that corresponds at least roughly to the outline you have been updating regularly.

Sort the cards into groups and consider any last-minute changes you might want to make in your outline before beginning the first draft. Don Schmidt, the student who was researching the Berlin Wall, realized that he had not been finding nearly as much material as he expected on the political effects of the wall. He had gotten particularly interested in the way the wall affected people personally, and the political effects seemed to be more on an international scale. The people who lived near the wall felt it more on an economic and social level. As a result, he changed his tentative outline to show only two main headings— the social effects and the economic effects of the wall.

Consider what kinds of natural groupings might exist with the cards you have. For instance, among his cards covering economic effects, Don saw natural groupings of long-term and short-term effects. His cards covering social effects fell naturally into groups dealing with the immediate family, the extended family, friends, and religion.

It is possible that you will have a few stray cards, ones that don't seem to fit in anywhere. Set them aside. You may find a use for them later, but don't squeeze them in just for the sake of including everything you know. The reader will never miss what doesn't really belong.

Write your first draft as quickly as possible. Don't be concerned about spelling, punctuation, and style. Get the ideas written out, even though you know changes will be necessary. By this time you know that revising is a lot easier than the original process of getting words down on paper. Also, be flexible. If new relationships or new ways to include interesting facts come to mind, use them. Your outline is a guide for the times when you don't know how to handle the information. If you get a better idea, go with it.

Don't forget to include in the margin the sources of your information. Nothing formal is needed at this point, but you should jot the author's name and the page numbers beside the text. Remember, if the author was not identified, use the title of the article. This information is at the bottom of your note card.

If you have no specific ideas for the introduction or the conclusion, ignore them for the time being. Writing them will be easier after you know exactly what you are introducing or concluding. If you want to get started, however, you could introduce the paper either by explaining why your topic is a significant issue or by telling how you became interested in it. You might conclude by summing up your feelings about the topic. In a typical research paper, you will not get many chances to include your own opinion, and the conclusion may be a good opportunity. Finally, any of the methods you learned in Chapter 2 would be appropriate to open or close your paper.

SUMMARY

Begin the writing process by organizing your note cards into the proper sequence. Set aside any extra cards and, working from your notes, write your first draft as quickly as you can. Be open to new ideas. Be scrupulous about recording sources in the margins. Don't worry about the introduction or the conclusion at this time.

DISCUSS

1. What is the purpose of organizing the note cards by their headings?
2. Besides organizing the cards according to their headings, what else might you accomplish by inspecting your note cards before starting to write?
3. In what way is the outline still tentative?

ACT

Following the steps discussed, write the first draft of your research paper. If you are writing your first draft by hand, double-space the text so that you can make additions or changes later.

Revising the First Draft

If you can possibly fit a one- or two-day break into your research paper schedule, this is a good time. You are going to be reading your own work. Putting a little time between writing and revising will make you much more objective.

When you wrote the first draft, you went as quickly as possible so there are bound to be changes needed. Don't try to find all of them the first time through. Give yourself a minimum of four readings so that you can devote your attention to one aspect of the paper at a time.

With each reading, you will be looking for some of the improvements discussed in Chapters 3 and 4. On your first reading, make sure the information is clear. You may need to add or delete material. Keep your notes handy and watch for confusing sections where the message you had in mind might not be coming through. Also be sure that your transitions show the relationships between various sections of your paper and how one sentence leads to another.

With the second reading, cut out any material that is off the subject or repetitious. Consult your outline. Does everything in the paper fit under one of the major headings? Have you included interesting but irrelevant material? If so, cut it.

Use a third reading to work toward the perfect combinations of words. You know that the first words down on paper can always be improved. Work on finding the most specific words possible, the most direct way of stating your meaning. Then go back and think about the variety, or lack of it, in your sentence structure.

Finally, see if any mechanical errors have slipped by you. You probably caught several small problems in the previous readings, but read your paper at least once more and try to make it as near perfect as possible.

SUMMARY

Try to take a day or two away from your paper. Then read it over several times. Check it for clarity, smooth transitions, repetition, word choice, sentence structure, and mechanical errors.

DISCUSS

1. What is the advantage of taking some time away from your paper before revising it?
2. Why is it unwise to try revising your paper all at once rather than in several small steps?

ACT

Go back to your first draft and read it over several times. On each reading, concentrate on a different area of improvement.

Preparing the Final Copy

After several readings and much revision, you are ready to prepare the final copy. Considering the time and effort you have put into it, this paper deserves a neat, polished presentation. If possible, it should be typed and double-spaced. If that is impossible, copy it neatly in ink.

The 1990s is a decade of change, and one big change in research papers involves the format used when you type that final copy. The more common use of word processors to compose research papers is encouraging many modifications. The latest Modern Language Association style reflects these changes and has been adopted in most high schools and colleges. Your teacher's preferences will be the final determiner but, in this evolutionary time, the following are generally accepted guidelines for typing the modern research paper.

Double-space, leaving a one-inch margin on all sides. Instead of a cover page, at the upper left of the first text page, type a heading that includes your name, your teacher's name, the course, and the due date of your paper. In the upper right-hand corner of each page after that, type your last name and the page number. Bind the pages together according to your teacher's directions. (Most teachers prefer a paper clip or staple rather than a plastic binder that will make your paper bulky and hard to handle.)

Any quotation of five or more lines should be set off in a paragraph by itself, and indented ten spaces from the left margin. Omit the quotation marks and continue to double-space. If the quote is just one paragraph, don't indent the first line more than the ten spaces.

The big change in research papers involves the method used to credit your sources. At one time, the only acceptable method was footnotes. Then endnotes—the same information put at the end of the paper—became popular. The latest variation (now the Modern Language Association standard) is called parenthetical, or internal, documentation because the source reference is inserted parenthetically into the text. Regardless of which form you use, a complete list of Works Cited will be included at the very end of the paper. Directions for all three methods are provided here.

Parenthetical Documentation

All parenthetical documentation directs the reader to the books or magazines listed as Works Cited at the end of your paper. Since complete bibliographic information is given there, the parentheses contain only the minimum information necessary to identify your source. The parenthetical reference should be inserted at the end of the sentence preceding the period.

Use the following illustrations as your guide.

1. Both the author's name and the page number are put in parentheses:

Being a Marine gave Oswald an identity (Reston 31).

This means that the information was found on page 31 of the book or magazine by Reston.

2. If the author's name has been included in the text, only the page number is needed in parentheses:

According to Reston, Oswald got his identity from being a Marine (31).

3. If a quotation comes at the end of a sentence, the parenthetical reference should be inserted between the closing quotation mark and the period:

"He did not like Connally, but he never said a word about Kennedy" (Reston 32).

Because of the special circumstances of parenthetical documentation, this contradicts the rule for end punctuation with quotations.

4.   If the quotation is long enough to be set off from the rest of the text, there will be no quotation marks. Place the parentheses two spaces after the period:

I feel that the reason he had Connally in his mind was on account of his discharge from the Marines and various letters they exchanged between the Marine Corps and the Governor's office, but actually, I didn't think that he had any idea concerning President Kennedy. (Reston 36)

Footnotes and Endnotes

Footnotes supply the same information as parenthetical documentation but, instead of looking back to the list of works cited, the reader has the complete reference at the bottom of the page. Endnotes take exactly the same form as footnotes except that they are all typed on a separate sheet at the end of the paper.

Footnotes and endnotes have the same purpose as parenthetical documentation. They tell the reader which of your sources supplied a piece of information. Instead of parentheses, however, you insert a number into the text. Type the number slightly above the line of text, following the end punctuation.

According to Reston, Oswald got his identity from being a Marine.[1]

The number *1* means that it is the first footnote and refers to a documentary note at the bottom of the page. Footnotes should be single-spaced, but double-space between each footnote if there are multiple entries on that page.

[1]James Reston, "Was Connally the Real Target?" *Time* November 28, 1988: 31.

The form for footnotes and endnotes changes depending on the type of source being credited. The footnote above was for a signed magazine article. Use the following examples as a guide for footnotes or endnotes.

1. For a book:

²David Lifton, *Best Evidence* (New York: Macmillan Publishing Co. Inc. 1980) 53.

2. For an unsigned magazine article:

³"John Kennedy's Death: The Debate Still Rages," *U.S. News and World Report* 21 Nov. 1983: 49.

3. For a signed newspaper article:

⁴George Henipen, "Kennedy's Death Remembered," *Cedar Rapids Gazette* 28 Nov. 1988: A2.

4. For an encyclopedia article:

⁵"Kennedy, John Fitzgerald," *Funk and Wagnalls New Encyclopedia,* Vol. 15: 205.

If you refer to the same source several times, you can save yourself some typing by using an abbreviated form. Retype only enough information to identify the source.

²David Lifton, *Best Evidence* (New York: Macmillan Publishing Co. Inc. 1980) 53.
²Lifton 56.

Even though the second reference was found on the same page as the first, the page number should be retyped. *Ibid.* and *op. cit.* are no longer recommended as references.

Works Cited

Whether you use parenthetical documentation, footnotes, or endnotes, you will also include an alphabetized, double-spaced list of works cited on the last page of your paper. Follow the form given in these examples.

1. A book:

Sparrow, John. *After the Assassination.* New York: Chilmark Press, 1967.

2. A signed magazine article:

Minnis, Jack. "Did the Mob Kill JFK?" *Time* 28 Nov. 1988: 42-49.

3. An unsigned magazine article:

"The Warren Commission; Testimony and Evidence." *Time* 4 Dec. 1964: 25-27.

4. A signed newspaper article:

Henipen, George. "Kennedy's Death Remembered." *Cedar Rapids Gazette* 28 Nov. 1988, early ed.: A2.

5. An unsigned newspaper article:

"Students Conduct Own Ceremony." *Cedar Rapids Gazette* 23 Nov. 1988, early ed.: A2.

6. An encyclopedia article:

"Kennedy, John Fitzgerald." *Funk and Wagnalls New Encyclopedia.* Vol. 15, p. 205.

DISCUSS

Read the following research paper and be prepared to answer the questions following it.

Sarah Kreykes
Ms. Ambrosina
Composition II
9 May 19____

Developing a Positive Self-Image

Self-esteem, as defined by Webster, is simply "belief in oneself." The development of a good self-concept is, however, a complex process. Most of us don't often think about our self-esteem levels. We probably don't know much about them, either, but self-esteem is an important factor in achieving personal happiness, quality relationships with others, and overall success (Buscaglia 28).

Self-concept starts forming early in childhood. Before kids start school, they begin to develop their ideas about the four components of self-value: body image, social self, cognitive self, and affecting self.

A child's body image is his or her sense of personal appearance and motor performance (Encyclopedia of Educational Research 484). Physical beauty, or lack of it, has enormous impact on the way people value themselves; even nursery school children are aware of their physical good points and flaws. Beautiful children are treated differently than ugly children. They get more attention, don't receive blame as often, and are disciplined less severely than unattractive youngsters. At an early age, kids pick up on society's message that being beautiful is socially important (Dobson 23-32). Physical appearance affects how children relate to others and how others relate to them. A little boy with a big nose or ears that stick out is bound to hear about it from his peers, or possibly from adults. In fact, dozens of children's stories center on the concept of beauty affecting relationships. *The Ugly Duckling, Sleeping Beauty, Rudolph the Red-nosed Reindeer, Dumbo the Elephant, Snow White and the Seven Dwarfs,* and *Cinderella* are just a few.

Social self is a child's sense of relationships. This includes the kinds of friendships, parent relationships, and teacher relationships children have, and how they feel about the communication and exchange of love going on within them.

The sense of ability to learn and solve problems is a child's cognitive self (E.E.R. 484). "Intelligence is another extremely critical attribute in evaluating the worth of a child, second only to beauty in importance," according to James Dobson, well-known author of several child-raising books (45). Most parents want their children to excel academically, and children sense that. They understand their intellectual abilities by the time they are five or six, shortly after entering school. Kids are compared to their classmates all the time, by adults and by each other. Teachers measure and compare abilities with different levels of reading groups, gold-star charts, spelling bees, and a number of other methods. Children want to be the best in their class because they know that intelligence is valuable.

The final component of a child's personality, affecting self, is the child's sense of ability to control or affect change in the environment (E.E.R. 484). Young children learn the sense of power they have when they assume leadership roles, and they enjoy that power. This is evident in watching kids play; they often fight over who gets to choose the game, and they love to boss each other around.

Self-esteem develops when a child measures the worth of his or her body image, social self, cognitive self, and affecting self, and comes up with a total self-value (E.E.R. 484). Inconsistencies in beauty, intelligence, and popularity can greatly sway children's opinions of themselves; early blunders and mistakes are remembered for years.

Other factors influence self-esteem, also. Society can play a part in molding a self-concept; the media and peers send out messages of what is acceptable in a person and what isn't (Dobson 13-19). Adults and older siblings crush a child's self-confidence with scornful comments and incessant teasing. Problems within the family unit, such as financial hardship and alcoholism, can make a child feel less valuable when she or he compares the family to other families. Disease or disability can make a young person feel "flawed" or "defective," and therefore not worth as much as another child (Dobson 53-54).

Though circumstances can greatly impair self-esteem in a young person, positive influences can balance the negative ones. Self-esteem is built in early childhood through the ways children are nurtured and loved by parents (Buscaglia 28). Children depend on their parents to supply their basic needs and to approve of them (Urquhart 50). They detect pride and respect, or disappointment and indifference, in their parents' manner. Significant people in a child's life foster self-esteem by accepting the child for who he or she is, by reinforcing uniqueness, by establishing in the child a sense of personal dignity, and by encouraging confidence (Buscaglia 28).

Teachers can also help children develop self-esteem. Recognizing a child's individuality while helping the child interact better with groups builds good self-concept. Teacher attitudes and classroom structures should enhance self-knowledge and positive feelings about school (E.E.R. 1233). An accepting, warm, empathetic, open, and nonjudgmental environment allows students to explore their thoughts and feelings about themselves (E.E.R. 448). Teachers should recognize children's academic successes and periodically remind them of their capabilities. Teachers should also help students in areas where they struggle and help them realize that a single failure does not make the whole person a failure.

Self-esteem exhibits itself in a number of ways. People with good self-concepts are happy. They "hold to firm beliefs in themselves, and though they may be concerned with what others think about them, their well-being does not depend on it," writes Leo Buscaglia (28). They aren't afraid to speak their minds, even if their opinions on a subject are unpopular. Why? Because people with high self-esteem respect themselves and give themselves enough credibility to stick by their feelings.

Typically, the people with good self-concepts are popular; they make wonderful friends. Relationships come easily for them because they're not afraid to go out on a limb to reach someone. Honesty, sincerity, and courage make them comfortable yet exciting to be around.

People with high self-esteem are generally successful in their careers and in other parts of their lives. They are not easily threatened by the future or changing circumstances because they know that they have the personal resources to meet whatever might confront them. They have confidence, the ultimate key to success (Buscaglia 28). Self-confident people face reality squarely and solve problems as they come along.

On the other end of the scale are the people with low self-esteem. Low self-esteem leads directly to unhappiness. People with poor self-concepts are likely to feel unworthy of love or rewards because they don't love themselves. They recognize only their flaws, and probably have forgotten that they have any strong points (Braiker 110). They have a tendency to dwell on, and perhaps stretch out of proportion, past mistakes and don't give themselves second chances.

Low self-esteem causes people to be unauthentic. Instead of letting their real personalities shine through, they squeeze themselves into molds to live up to someone else's standards. They think that who they really are is unacceptable. The tragic part of living unauthentically is that this negative process builds on itself. Trying to be a different person makes self-esteem sink lower because the real personality is rejected and negative characteristics are emphasized (Branden 130).

People with low self-esteem often do not feel any joy or sense of accomplishment in reaching goals (Urquhart 50). In fact, many times they just assume that they set their goals too low or set the wrong goals. They are incapable of feeling pride in themselves, and constantly feel like failures. The positive success cycle corresponds with a negative failure cycle; one failure puts an end to any further attempts. If people are not trying, they cannot succeed.

Low self-esteem has been cited as the cause for a number of problems affecting both individuals and large groups of people. It is a chief cause of bad relationships; people can't give love if they don't feel it for themselves first. Thousands of broken marriages are the result of people not being able to relate to each other; their poor self-concepts get in the way of honesty and good communication (Braiker 110). Low self-esteem has also been blamed for the widespread teenage abuse of drugs and alcohol. Teenagers don't have the self-confidence to "just say no" because they fear rejection from their peers. Their self-worth is too wrapped up in the opinions of others. Low self-esteem also causes kids to drop out of school when they get overwhelmed by the challenges and feel that they can't handle the pressure (Braiker 110).

Another problem stemming from low self-esteem is anorexia. Anorexia is "a psychological and endocrinal disorder that is characterized by a pathological fear of weight gain leading to faulty eating patterns, malnutrition, and excessive weight loss" (Franklin 41). The disease usually affects young females, but more male cases are being noticed these days. Anorexic girls are not happy with who they are or with how their lives are going, so they stop eating to gain control over some fraction of their existence. They find, though, that losing weight doesn't give them more confidence; instead, they continue to feel fat, no matter how thin they become. They feel inadequate because love (from other people and from themselves) is conditional on achievement, and they cannot achieve the ideal body (Franklin 42).

Thus, high self-esteem is something to work toward. Many people have realized the importance of a sense of self-worth and have devised ways to improve self-concept. One

very basic step toward improving self-esteem is to live authentically. Projecting a real image builds self-respect because people are accepting themselves. According to
Nathaniel Branden, there are four steps to becoming more
authentic. The first step is for people to meditate on the lies
they are living, but avoid guilt feelings; self-understanding
is built in this manner. Second, they should imagine explaining the reason for those lies to a compassionate friend;
this makes clear the survival value of the fake image. The
third step to building self-image with Branden's plan is to
imagine acting real in a specific situation; people ask themselves, "How do I feel? How are others reacting to me?" The
final step is to rethink the living-authentically scenario on a
daily or weekly basis to build confidence. If people discover
why it's hard to be honest, they can get rid of their urge to
be dishonest (Branden 130-137).

Leo Buscaglia has created another approach, a seven-
step plan for building self-esteem. He says that "if you want
others to love you, learn to love yourself" (28). The first
thing people must do to learn to love themselves is to accept
who they are. Trying to change themselves is time wasted,
so efforts are better directed toward developing the unique
person who already exists. The second step to build more
positive feelings is to work toward fulfilling their potential.
"There are no limits to what we can become in a single lifetime," Buscaglia says (28). We shouldn't stay in comfortable
roles but should try to improve ourselves.

Appreciating the personality that exists is the third step
to developing a better self-concept; people need to realize
what they have to offer others. The fourth step is to give
themselves love and understanding. Buscaglia says it's not
egocentric or immature for people to make themselves the
center of their lives. Forgiving mistakes, being real, and
making their own definitions of self are the last three steps
to having better self-esteem. Buscaglia agrees with Branden
and notes that fake roles take away energy that could be in-
vested in personal growth. He also says, "*We* are the only
ones who have a right to assess, define, and defend who we
are" (Buscaglia 28, 31).

Gilbert Brim has a slightly different approach. He says
that sometimes a bit of a challenge and a sense of autonomy
are what it takes to increase people's satisfaction with their

achievements and with themselves. However, many are already performing at, or near, capacity. Challenge is not what they need to develop a better self-concept. They need to learn to work only to the "just manageable difficulty" level, and learn to manage their achievement gaps. Management of achievement gaps is the process of arranging and managing lives to keep a balance between achievement and capacity. People need to create a balance by resetting goals in response to wins and losses.

People naturally manage their achievement gaps in response to failures. They first search for better ways to complete the task they failed at. Then they try extending their timetable for achieving the goal. Next they reduce their standards of quality and, finally, forgo unrealistic goals. Men and women subconsciously go through a similar process in response to successes: When they are successful, they often shorten their timetables for other goals, raise their quality expectations, and add new goals to the list (Brim 48-52).

Brim concludes that "people are designed to deal with winning and losing; we have all kinds of weapons to deal with failure and success and remain on an even keel" (52). To develop and maintain self-esteem, people must be realistic about what they can accomplish and take pride in what they do accomplish.

In the past five or ten years, a great deal of research has been done on the importance of self-esteem, and people are beginning to take notice of the significance of having a good self-concept. In California, the state legislature formed a committee to study self-esteem. Even though the idea was not universally popular, Governor George Deukmejian told the *Los Angeles Times* that "everybody knows the social costs of low self-esteem to be incalculable" (Seligman 101).

California's Task Force to Promote Self-esteem and Personal and Social Responsibility released a statement of goals in its newsletter, Esteem:

We seek to determine whether self-esteem and personal and social responsibility are the keys to unlocking the secrets of healthy human development so that we can get to the roots of and develop effective solutions for major social problems; to develop and provide for every Californian the latest knowledge and practices regarding the significance of self-esteem, and personal and social responsibility. (California Esteemin' 16)

The four goals cited in the statement were to research self-esteem, to propose a plan to promote good self-esteem through government and private institutions and the news media, to provide the public with information about self-esteem, and to set up locally based task forces to investigate and promote self-esteem (California Esteemin' 16).

John Vasconellos, the Democratic assemblyman who created the California task force, wanted to set up the self-esteem group because of his personal experiences in counseling, encounter groups, stress management courses, and seminars at the Esalen Institute. He said:

Self-esteem is implicated as the causal factor in crime, drug abuse, child abuse, and chronic welfare dependency. Idealistically, this task force will let people know where to go for help and how to begin practicing truly nurturing self-esteem. (Faber 32)

Self-esteem can be compared to an eggshell, one of nature's finer bits of engineering. If the ends of the elliptical shell are squeezed, it is nearly unbreakable. However, an egg can be easily broken if treated carelessly. Self-esteem is like that eggshell. It can be a fragile thing, damaged by words or actions. But it can also be exceptionally strong, almost unbreakable. People need to love and respect themselves; it's the chief means of strengthening their delicate shells and leading happier lives. Nurturing self-esteem is not a triviality. It is the key to a meaningful life.

Works Cited

Braiker, Harriet. "How to Feel Better about Yourself." *McCall's* Sept. 1988: 110-112.

Branden, Nathaniel. "Living Authentically: The Key to Self-esteem." *Cosmopolitan* Mar. 1987: 130-137.

Brim, Gilbert. "Losing and Winning." *Psychology Today* Sept. 1988: 48-52.

Buscaglia, Leo. "There's No One in the World Like You." *Woman's Day* 29 Mar. 1988: 28-31.

"California Esteemin'." *Harper's Magazine* Aug. 1987: 16.

Dobson, James. *Hide or Seek.* Old Tappan, New Jersey: Fleming H. Revell Company, 1979.

Encyclopedia of Educational Research. New York: Macmillan and Free Press, 1982.

Faber, Nancy. "Okay, We Make Fun of California; Now the State Is Putting Money Where Its Mouth Is. Yikes!" *People Weekly* 2 Mar. 1987: 32-34.

Franklin, Neshama. "Starved for Self-esteem." *Medical Self Care* Summer 1985: 41+.

Seligman, Daniel. "Touchy-Feely-Dopey." *Fortune* 20 July 1987: 101.

Urquhart, Paulette. "How to Improve Your Self-esteem." *Chatelaine* April 1988: 50.

DISCUSS

1. What is the difference between footnotes and endnotes? List the advantages and disadvantages of each.
2. Describe parenthetical documentation. How is it more informative than endnotes? Is it less informative than footnotes? What advantages does it have for both writer and reader?

ACT

Prepare the final copy of your research paper according to your teacher's directions.

A Handbook of Style

In Chapter 1 you read a story about President Truman and his writing problem. He never admitted defeat, but the problem plagued him through life and was a constant irritation. Most important, though, he was aware of the problem and did something about it.

Most people troubled by style and usage problems can find help in the definitions, explanations, and examples that follow. Look them over and use this guide as the need arises. You may even want to add some of them to your journal.

a, an. **A** goes in front of words that begin with a consonant sound. **An** goes in front of words beginning with a vowel sound. Sound, not spelling, determines the correct form.

a hospital   an honor
a dictionary   an envelope
a use   an office

accept, except. **Accept** means "to receive willingly." **Except** means either "excluding" or "omit."

Joe accepted the trophy.
Everyone except Joe missed the ceremony.
Question number twelve will be excepted from the test.

adapt, adopt. **Adapt** means "change to fit the circumstances." **Adopt** means "to take as your own."

Terry will adapt to his new job.
The school will adopt new textbooks.

advice, advise. **Advice** means "guidance." **Advise** means "to offer advice."

Jim gave me a good piece of advice.
I would advise you to drive carefully.

affect, effect. **Affect** is a verb meaning "to influence." **Effect** can be used either as a noun meaning "a consequence," or as a verb meaning "to accomplish."

The fire affected our class schedule.
The fire had no effect on any of the occupants.
The President effected changes in foreign policy.

ain't. **Ain't** is still used in some informal speech, but it is almost always considered an uneducated usage. In writing (except for dialogue), always use **isn't**.

all ready, already. **All ready** means "all are prepared." **Already** means "previously."

The boys were all ready to march out the door.
He already finished the assignment.

all right, alright. Although **alright** is becoming more common, **all right** is still preferred for all meanings. Use **all right**.

allusion, illusion. **Allusion** means "a reference to someone or something." **Illusion** means "a misconception or a false impression."

His allusion to *Hamlet* impressed Jennifer.
She is under the illusion that he is intelligent.

all together, altogether. **All together** means "all in the same place." **Altogether** means "entirely."

I fixed it by putting the pieces all together.
The number of students is altogether too high.

a lot, alot, allot. **A lot** may be used to mean "a large number or amount," and it must be spelled as two words. **Allot** means "to apportion." Do not use **alot**.

Hal gave me a lot of trouble.
The President will allot five minutes for each speech.

allude, refer. **Allude** means "to mention indirectly." **Refer** means "to mention directly."

Though he didn't mention a name, we all knew which student Mr. Kyle alluded to.
The candidate referred to her opponents by name when she talked about abuses of power.

among, between. **Among** is used to refer to three or more items. **Between** is used to refer to only two items.

The tickets were divided among the graduates.
She had to choose between the Chevy and the Ford.

Between may be used with more than two items if they are being considered as individuals, not as a group.

Between Jim, Lynette, and Toni, they managed to get the work completed.

amount of, number of. **Amount of** is used when referring to bulk quantities or heaps of things. **Number of** is used when referring to things that can be counted.

We carried a large amount of gravel in the truck.
Jody collected a number of signatures on her petition.

anxious, eager. **Anxious** means "extreme uneasiness or fear." **Eager** means "looking forward to something." The two are often confused.

Annette is anxious about meeting her in-laws.
Doug is eager to see Disney World.

apostrophe. The apostrophe is used to show possession, to form contractions, and to form some plurals.

Possessives:

1.   Singular nouns form the possessive by adding **'s**.

The book's cover fell off in my hands.

2.   Plural nouns ending in **s** form the possessive by adding only the apostrophe, after the **s**.

The students' lunchroom is a total disaster.

3.   Plural nouns not ending in **s** form the possessive by adding **'s.**

Women's clothing is entirely too expensive.

Contractions:

Contractions are written with an apostrophe replacing the omitted letters.

We're not going to be on time.
I shouldn't let him get away with eating so much.

Plurals:

Plurals of figures, letters, symbols, and words when used as words are formed by adding **'s.**

Steve got three *A's* last semester.
I used too many *however's* in the last essay.

black, white. When **black** and **white** are used to indicate race, they are not capitalized. **African-American, Afro-American, Caucasian,** and **Negro** are capitalized.

borrow, lend. A person who **borrows** "gets." A person who **lends** "gives."

Tim borrowed Nancy's car. (Tim got the use of the car.)
The bank lends money to people. (The bank distributes the money.)

brake, break. **Brake** means "slowing something" or "a means of slowing something." **Break** means "to fracture" something.

> Step on the brakes.
> Terri threatened to break the window.

bust. **Bust** is usually considered a nonstandard form of **break** or **burst.** The term **drug bust,** referring to a police raid, is now so commonly used that it may be considered standard.

can, may. **Can** refers to "ability." **May** refers to "permission."

> We can run the entire race in under six minutes.
> May I borrow your jacket?

capital, capitol. **Capital** has many possible meanings. Among them are "uppercase letters," "the city where laws are made," and "punishment resulting in death." **Capitol** refers only to "the building where the legislature meets."

> Capitalize the first letter of the sentence.
> The capital of Iowa is Des Moines.
> I don't believe in capital punishment.
> The capitol is topped with a golden dome.

capitalization.
1. Capitalize the first word in a sentence, a quotation, or a line of poetry.

> George asked, "Do you think Janie is a terrible driver?"

2. Capitalize proper nouns, including titles used with names.

> Jeff drove all the way from Chicago in his Chevy.
> The parade was led by Grand Marshall Atwood.

3. Capitalize days of the week, months, and holidays.

> This year Easter falls on the third Sunday of April.

4. Capitalize the most important words in the titles of books, plays, short stories, poems, and chapters.

A Twist of the Wrist was written by Keith Code.

censor, censure. **Censor** refers to "a person who controls what other people see," or "the act of prohibiting." **Censure** means "condemn."

The censor cut the third scene out of the movie.
The city council doesn't want to censor any magazines.
Council members voted to censure the mayor's misuse of power.

choose, chose. **Choose** means "to pick." It is the present tense. **Chose** is the past tense of choose.

Choose your weapons.
Yesterday they chose their weapons.

cite, site, sight. **Cite** means "refer to." **Site** is a "place" or "location." **Sight** is "the ability to see," or "a view."

When doing research, always remember to cite your authority.
That hill is the proposed site of the new church.
The surgery restored Uncle George's sight.
The explosion was quite a sight.

clothes, cloths. **Clothes** are "what you wear." **Cloths** are "pieces of fabric."

His clothes were appropriate for the occasion.
The cleaning cloths were green and blue.

coarse, course. **Coarse** means "rough texture." **Course** refers to a "plan of action, movement, or study."

Use three pounds of coarse sand.
We played on a nine-hole golf course.

colon.
1. Use a colon to introduce an explanation, amplification, or summary of what has come before.

The earthquake was devastating: more than 1,700 people were left homeless.

2. Use a colon to introduce a long quotation.
3. Use a colon to introduce a list.

Common coordinating conjunctions are *and, but, or,* and *nor.*

comma.
1. Use a comma in a compound sentence before the coordinating conjunction.

Wayne Rainey holds many speed records, but Eddie Lawson beats him regularly.

2. Use a comma to set off parenthetical expressions and nouns of direct address.

You will, of course, go to the seminar. Won't you, John?

3. Use a comma to separate items in a series.

The desk, chair, lamp, and table all bounced down the stairs.

4. Use a comma after introductory phrases and clauses.

To understand her, you have to listen very closely.
On the shelf in the closet, my trophy gathers dust.
If you want to go along, you'll need to get shots and a passport within the next few days.

5. Use a comma to set off nonessential modifiers.

Mike Hayes, who lives across the street, is a patrolman.

Since you know Mike is a patrolman, the clause ''who lives across the street'' is nonessential and is set off by commas.
Modifiers essential to the meaning of the sentence are not set off by commas.

The man who lives across the street is a patrolman.

In this case, "who lives across the street" is essential to identifying which patrolman. Therefore, it is not set off by commas.

6. Use a comma to set off appositives when they are only giving additional information, not identifying the noun they refer to.

Jerry Duea, a good talker, is the tallest boy on the team.

When the appositive is necessary to identify the noun, do not use commas.

The book *Blue Highways* is about one man's tour of America.

7. Use a comma when necessary for clarity.

To Joyce, William's party was a bore.

The comma prevents the sentence from being read, "To Joyce William's party. . . ."

8. Use a comma to separate items in dates and addresses.

On August 21, 1990, the restaurant was reopened at 2344 University Avenue, Waterloo, Iowa.

complected, complexioned. **Complected** is used occasionally in such phrases as "a light-complected man." **Complexioned** is still the preferred form.

Her whole family is light complexioned.

complement, compliment. **Complement** is "the number that makes something complete." **Compliment** is "an expression of admiration."

At its full complement, the team has twelve players.
Mr. Kelly complimented Kay on her beautiful photograph.

continual, continuous. The meanings are similar, but not identical. **Continual** means "repeatedly." **Continuous** means "uninterrupted."

Becoming a good motorcycle rider calls for continual practice.
The roar of the crowd was continuous.

could of, should of, would of. These should be **could have,
should have,** and **would have.** Or, informally, **could've,
should've,** and **would've.** In speech, the words may sound
like "of," but, when you are writing, spell them out.

council, counsel, consul. **Council** means "an elected assembly."
Counsel means "to advise." **Consul** is "an official who represents our interests in another country."

The city council meets on Monday evening.
Ms. Jones was available to counsel students about careers.
Mr. McRea tried to get appointed consul to Yugoslavia.

criteria, criterion. **Criteria** is the plural form of **criterion.**

What is your first criterion?
My criteria are too numerous to list.

dangling modifier. A dangling modifier is one that seems to modify the wrong word. The modifier in the next sentence is dangling because it seems to modify the word **expenses.**

Being high school seniors, college expenses are a major interest for
all of us.

Logically, college expenses cannot be high school seniors. In
the next sentence, the modifier seems to refer to the word
mountain. Of course, the mountain could not drive along at
any speed.

Driving along at 65 mph, the mountain came quickly into view.

Sentences with dangling modifiers are best improved by a
complete rewriting.

Since we are high school seniors, college expenses are a major
interest.
We were driving along at 65 mph when the mountain came into
view.

desert, dessert. **Desert,** with the accent on the first syllable, means "a barren area." With the accent on the second syllable, **desert** means "leave." **Dessert** always means "the last part of a meal, a treat."

Barstow is in the middle of the Mohave desert.
If you desert, you are classified A.W.O.L.
We had pie for dessert.

discover, invent. **Discover** means "to gain knowledge of something that already exists." **Invent** means "to think up and bring into existence something that did not exist before."

Louis Pasteur discovered that microorganisms were the cause of fermentation.
Eli Whitney invented the cotton gin in 1793.

discreet, discrete. **Discreet** describes someone who is "tactful." **Discrete** means "individually distinct."

The detective was very discreet in looking for evidence.
The discrete pieces of evidence, together, formed a convincing argument.

disinterested, uninterested. **Disinterested** means "impartial." **Uninterested** means "indifferent."

We need to find disinterested judges for the contest.
Terri was uninterested in the possibility of a new job.

due to. Usually a symptom of wordiness, the phrase is frowned upon. Even if **due to** seems the shortest form, avoid it.

Avoid: Due to the loud noise, I got a headache.
Better: The loud noise gave me a headache.
Or even: Because of the loud noise, I got a headache.

dyeing. dying. **Dyeing** means "changing the color of something. **Dying** means "losing life."

Theresa is dyeing her shoes blue.
Dying is an important part of the life process.

eminent, imminent. Eminent means "distinguished." **Imminent** means "likely to happen soon."

Dr. Phaltzgraff is an eminent historian from the university.
The imminent danger of explosion caused near panic.

enormity, enormousness. Enormity means "atrociousness" or "outrageousness." **Enormousness** means "extraordinary size."

We were shocked by the enormity of the violent crime.
The enormousness of the birthday cake was overwhelming.

etc. Etc. is an abbreviation for the Latin term **et cetera,** which means "and others." It is generally accepted in informal speech but should be avoided in writing. **Etc.** is often viewed as a method of pretending you could give more detail when you really can't think of any additional facts.

everyday, every day. Everyday means "ordinary." **Every day** means "each day."

You perform everyday duties every day.

farther, further. Farther means "a greater distance." **Further** means "to a greater degree or extent."

Denver is fifteen miles farther.
We'll discuss this further before making a decision.

fewer, less. Fewer refers to "number of individual units." It is used with nouns that can be counted. **Less** refers to "quantity." It is used with nouns that can be measured but not counted separately.

The quiet weekend meant less traffic.
As a result, fewer accidents took place.

flaunt, flout. **Flaunt** means "to show off." **Flout** means "to treat with scorn."

The dowager flaunted her diamond jewelry.
Sunday drivers flout every traffic law.

formally, formerly. **Formally** means "marked by ceremony." **Formerly** means "previously."

Has the President been formally introduced?
Mr. Lewis formerly worked at the packing plant.

former, latter. **Former** means "the first of a pair that was mentioned." **Latter** means "the second of the pair mentioned."

The Corvette and Thunderbird were similar in the 1950s, but the former developed into a sports car. The latter became a family car.

good, well. **Good** is an adjective, which modifies nouns or pronouns. **Well** is an adverb, which modifies verbs.

He did a good job.
She types well.

Well is also used after the linking verbs **be, feel,** and **seem** when you are referring to "good health."

He felt pretty well after a day of rest.

hanged, hung. **Hanged** is the past tense of **hang** meaning to execute. **Hung** is the past tense of **hang** meaning to suspend.

They hanged the traitor at sunrise.
We hung the balloons from the ceiling.

healthful, healthy. Although often used interchangeably, these words have distinct meanings that are preferred in formal writing. **Healthful** means "good for a person's health." **Healthy** means "having or seeming to be in good health."

Bicycling is a healthful form of recreation.
With all her walking, Jean is bound to be healthy.

Informally, **healthy** is often used to mean "big."

She receives a healthy allowance every week.

hear, here. **Hear** means "to use the ears." **Here** means "this location."

Did you hear the blast?
The books are over here on the table.

hole, whole. **Hole** means "an opening." **Whole** means "complete," or "entire."

The hole was seven feet deep.
We ate the whole melon.

hopefully. **Hopefully** should be used only in an adverb position to mean "in a hopeful way."

Fido waited hopefully for a crumb to fall on the floor.

Often, **hopefully** is used as an introductory word to mean "it is hoped."

Hopefully, Barney has a chance at the title.

Since the introductory **hopefully** is frowned on by many people, it would be better to replace it with "I hope," or "We hope."

imply, infer. **Imply** means "to indicate without stating directly." **Infer** means "to figure out." The writer **implies,** the reader **infers.**

Justin implied that the game was crooked.
By reading between the lines, we can infer that life was difficult for the author's family.

incomplete sentence. See sentence fragments.

irregardless. **Irregardless** is probably a combination of **irrespective** and **regardless.** Whatever its source, most people consider it nonstandard, even for informal speech. Use **regardless.**

it's, its, its'. **It's** means "it is." **Its** is the possessive form of **it. Its'** is never correct.

It's a good time to take a vacation.
The cat grooms its fur.

lay, lie. **Lay** means "to place or put." Its forms are **lay, laying,** and **laid.**

Lay the map on the table.
He is laying the tablecloth upside down.
They laid the carpet yesterday.
They had laid the asphalt by noon.

Lie means "to recline or stay in a position." Its forms are **lie, lying, lay, lain.**

The dog lies in the middle of the street all day.
Jim is lying in the hammock.
The dishes lay scattered all over the floor.
They have lain there since noon.

lead, led, lead. **Lead** means "to go first." **Led** is the past tense of the verb **to lead. Lead,** the noun, is a heavy metal.

You will lead the parade.
He led the parade yesterday.
The anchor was made of lead.

like, as. Strictly speaking, **like** should be used only as a preposition, not as a conjunction.

Mr. Modesto looks like an author.
Suzy laughs like her mother.
It seems as if we have been through this before.

literally. **Literally** is overused to emphasize statements. "We literally bombed them off the court." It should be avoided in situations where you are actually speaking figuratively.

loose, lose. **Loose** means "free, not tight." **Lose** means "to misplace something."

Never wear loose clothing around machinery.
Kids always lose their mittens.

media, medium. **Media,** often used in the sense of "the news media" or "communication media," is the plural of **medium.** As such, it takes a plural verb. Avoid the use of "mediums" or "medias."

Television is a popular entertainment medium.
The news media are often accused of inaccurate reporting.

miner, minor. A **miner** is "a worker in a mine." A **minor** is "someone under legal age," or "something comparatively unimportant."

You can expect a coal miner to be dirty.
Minors are not allowed where alcohol is served.
The leak is a minor irritation.

moral, morale. **Moral** means "good" or "lesson." **Morale** means a "mental state."

She is a moral person.
We knew the moral of the story.
Morale among the soldiers was high.

notorious, famous. **Notorious** has nearly the same definition as **famous,** but there is a crucial difference. **Famous** means "widely known" and has a positive connotation, while **notorious** means "widely known in an unfavorable way."

Sharon's uncle was a famous athlete when he was young.
Sam's uncle, I'm afraid, was a notorious bank robber.

parallelism. Parts of a sentence that serve similar functions should be similar in form. The following sentences are lacking parallelism.

Jim is friendly, helpful, and a generous person.
Riding the escalator is easier than when you take the elevator.
Reading, listening, and the ability to make inferences are all important communication skills.

If you want to help out, one could always make a financial contribution.

These sentences can be improved by using similar grammatical forms.

Jim is friendly, helpful, and generous.
Riding the escalator is easier than taking the elevator.
Reading, listening, and inferring are all important communication skills.
If you want to help out, you could always make a financial contribution.

passed, past. **Passed** is the past tense of the verb **to pass,** meaning "to hand" or "take a position in front of." **Past** is the correct form for all other uses, whether noun, adjective, or preposition.

Terri passed the other runners. (verb)
We passed the cake down to Ellie. (verb)
He was ashamed of his past. (noun)
Hal is a past-president of the student senate. (adjective)
He went right past the theater. (preposition)

peace, piece. **Peace** means "calm" or "the opposite of war." **Piece** means "a part of something."

The peace of the countryside calmed Jack's nerves.
Take a big piece of pizza.

personal, personnel. **Personal** means "individual." **Personnel** means "employees."

We all have our personal problems.
All part-time personnel received raises last year.

plain, plane. **Plain** means "simple, not fancy." **Plane** means "an airplane, a tool, or a flat surface."

Make mine plain; leave the whipped cream off.
The plane cruised at 10,000 feet.
Carpenters use a plane to smooth wood.
Plane Geometry is difficult.

principal, principle. A **principal** is "the head of a school." A **principle** is "a basic rule of conduct."

The principal of this school is your pal.
He believed in the principle of citizen participation.

quiet, quit, quite. **Quiet** means "silent." **Quit** means "stop." **Quite** means "wholly or completely."

The house was quiet after midnight.
Quit making that racket.
Are you quite finished?

quotation marks.

1. Use quotation marks to enclose the exact words of a speaker or another writer.

"The car," Andy said, "was moving too fast."
About lotteries, George Will says, "Thus do states simultaneously cheat and corrupt their citizens."

2. Use quotation marks for titles of stories, articles, chapters, short poems, and songs.

One of Faulkner's best-known short stories is "The Bear."
Marcy Krumm read Edna St. Vincent Millay's poem "Dirge Without Music."

3. Use single quotation marks for a quotation inside another quotation.

I told her, "If you never learn to say 'please' or 'thank you,' life is going to be awfully unpleasant."

4. Put commas and periods inside closing quotation marks. Put semicolons and colons outside closing quotation marks. Question marks are put inside the closing quotation mark if the quoted material is a question. Otherwise, question marks follow the closing quotation mark.

"This has too much salt," said Tammi.

She said, "Pass the bread, please."

The bus driver said, "Stay in your seats"; and when we tried to get up, he slammed on the brakes.

These runners were listed as "highly improved": Beth Graff, Nancy Groves, and Erin Phillips.

Jerry asked, "Are you going with us?"

Did you hear him say, "Time out"?

5. If a quotation continues for more than one paragraph, put opening quotation marks at the beginning of each paragraph, but close the quotation marks only at the end of the last paragraph.

raise, rise. **Raise** means "to lift up," "to rear," or "to collect." Its forms are **raise, raised,** and **raised. Rise** means "to get up." Its forms are **rise, rose,** and **risen.**

Mr. Pauly always raises his flag on federal holidays.

My grandmother raised seven children alone.

The class raised enough money for a post-prom party.

I never rise before noon if I can help it.

reason is because. "**The reason is because** he doesn't feel comfortable at parties," and "**The reason** he won't come **is because** he doesn't feel comfortable at parties," are both awkward and redundant constructions. "He won't come because he doesn't feel comfortable at parties" is much more direct and economical. Avoid the **reason is because.**

run-on sentences. When you put two independent clauses into one sentence, you ordinarily join them with either a comma and a coordinating conjunction, or a semicolon. A relative pronoun can also be used to join the clauses. If you use a comma alone, or use no punctuation at all, you have a run-on sentence.

Run-on sentences:

I got the dictionary, it settled the discussion quickly.

Get an early start, traffic will be terrible tomorrow.

We met our new neighbor, he is the one who built a fence.

Corrected sentences:
I got the dictionary, and it settled the discussion quickly.
Get an early start; traffic will be terrible tomorrow.
We met our new neighbor who built the fence.

semicolon.

1. Use a semicolon to connect independent clauses that are very closely related.

Kerri is admired by everyone; she can be depended on.

2. Use a semicolon to separate items in a series if any of the items contains a comma.

In the last three days, we have been to St. Louis, Missouri; Des Moines, Iowa; Omaha, Nebraska; and Springfield, Illinois.

3. Use a semicolon to separate independent clauses of a compound sentence joined by **and, but, or,** or **for** if one or both of the clauses contain a comma.

When the plant got dry, we watered it; but after that it drooped, withered, and died.

sentence fragments. Occasionally, a group of words that does not make a grammatical sentence is punctuated as if it were complete. These are called sentence fragments, or incomplete sentences.

We walked into the restaurant. And noticed that the place was nearly empty.
When we accelerated onto the freeway. The police car was still behind us.

Sentence fragments should be corrected either by joining them with other sentences or by completely rewriting them.

We walked into the restaurant, and noticed that the place was nearly empty.

or

We walked into the restaurant. The place was nearly empty.
When we accelerated onto the freeway, the police car was still behind us.

or: We accelerated onto the freeway with the police car still behind us.

If used only occasionally, the sentence fragment can be an effective means of emphasis.

Only a few years ago, people could rely on the safety of the cold, clear, pure water that flowed into their homes. Not now.

set, sit. **Set** means "to put or place something." Its principle parts are **set, set,** and **set.** It usually takes a direct object. **Sit** means "to occupy a place." Its principle parts are **sit, sat,** and **sat.** It almost never takes a direct object.

We set the table near the door.
Set all of your books on the shelf.
Amy could sit over there on the couch.
The school sits on seven acres of grassy hillside.

Set has a few unusual uses that do not mean "to put or place."

The sun sets in the west.
Set your watch for daylight-saving time.
Joe set a new record in Saturday's race.
The farmer kept over three hundred setting hens.

shone, shown. **Shone** is the past tense of "to shine." **Shown** is the past tense of "to show."

The floor shone after it was waxed.
The movie was shown at 3:00.

stationary, stationery. **Stationary** means "in a fixed position." **Stationery** means "writing paper."

The paint factory machinery was stationary.
I bought Margaret some monogrammed stationery.

subject-verb agreement.
    1.   A singular verb is used with a singular subject, and a plural verb is used with a plural subject.

An occasional accident **is** to be expected.
Accidents **are** to be expected.

2. When two subjects are connected by **and**, the verb must be plural.

Adam **walks** to school every day.
Adam and Sharon **walk** to school every day.

3. When two subjects are connected by **or, nor,** or **but,** the verb must be singular.

Either John or Manuel **has** a new Corvette.

4. When a modifier separates the subject and verb, the verb must agree with the true subject.

That pile of books **belongs** in the closet.
The books on the floor **belong** in the closet.

5. Some pronouns give the impression of being plural when they are actually singular. Examples are **everyone, nobody, everybody, anybody, either,** and **neither.**

Everyone is confused this morning.
Neither of them **wants** to leave early.

6. When collective nouns refer to a single unit, a singular verb must be used. When collective nouns refer to individuals acting separately, a plural verb must be used. A collective noun is one that names a group of persons or things. Examples are *audience, chorus, crowd, congregation, team, and jury.*

The **faculty is** meeting after school tonight.
The **faculty are** arguing about the new class schedule.

7. In a few sentence constructions, the subject comes after the verb. Subject and verb must still agree in number.

There **are** good **seats** left for Saturday's performance.
Here **are** the best **seats** in the house.
Have the **games** been played yet?

supposed to, suppose to. **Supposed to** is the correct form. The **d** sound at the end often disappears in speech, but the correct spelling does not change.

than, then. **Than** is used in comparison. **Then** means "next," or "at that time."

He is uglier than his dog.
Bring to a boil; then add the salt.
We left then.

their, there, they're. **Their** is the possessive form of "they." **There** means a "location." **They're** is the contraction for "they are."

Their car is blue.
We all go there for vacation.
They're going to join us later.

threw, through. **Threw** is the past tense of "to throw." **Through** means "from one side to the other."

He threw the ball through the window.

till, until, 'til. Both **until** and **till** are correct spellings. Do not use **'til.**

Do we have to wait until after school?
I can't wait till Christmas.

to, too, two. **To** means "in the direction of." **Too** means "also," or "more than necessary." **Two** means "more than one, less than three."

Give it to me.
I had some too; it was too much.
Two girls shared the prize.

underlining (italics).
   1. In handwritten and typed materials, underline words that are to be printed in italics.

   2.   Underline names of books, magazines, newspapers, movies, and works of art.

Life has a story on the Kentucky Derby.
Bing Crosby and Rosemary Clooney starred in ***White Christmas***.

   3.   Underline words used as words, letters used as letters, and numbers used as numbers.

You used *I* 37 times in your essay.
Uri got three *A*'s this semester.
Linda is four and she still confuses the numerals *6* and *9*.

unique. **Unique** means "the only one of its kind" and "cannot be compared." Thus, it is incorrect to describe something as being "more unique" than something else or "most unique." On the other hand, if the thing you are describing is one of a few, you could say "almost unique," or "nearly unique."

used to, use to. **Used to** is the correct form. The **d** sound at the end often disappears in speech, but the correct spelling does not change.

We used to go bowling every weekend.

verb forms. See subject-verb agreement.

waist, waste. **Waist** means "the midsection." **Waste** means "squander," or "leftover materials."

She had long legs and a tiny waist.
Don't waste your money.

weather, whether. **Weather** means "the climate." **Whether** shows doubt.

The weather was cold and rainy.
I couldn't tell whether he was finished.

who's, whose. **Who's** is the contraction for "who is." **Whose** is the possessive form of "who."

Who's going to the dance?
Whose dog is this?

-wise. Avoid using **-wise** as a suffix. Terms like gradewise, pointwise, and participationwise are always frowned upon.

your, you're. **Your** is the possessive form of "you." **You're** is the contraction of "you are."

Your dog is outside.
You're getting to be well known.

Proofreading Symbols

agr	agreement error	RO	run-on sentence
ap	apostrophe error	sp	spelling error
ante	antecedent not clear	S-V	subject-verb agreement
awk	awkward wording	trans	transition needed or weak
inc	incomplete sentence	TS	topic sentence
cap	capitalize	WC	word choice
dict	check definition in dictionary	WF	word form
lc	lower case	WW	wrong word
paral	make parallel	¶	paragraph needed
quo	add or correct quotation marks	no ¶	no paragraph needed
red	redundant	^	omission, word left out
		o	other miscellaneous errors

Index

NTC LANGUAGE ARTS BOOKS

Business Communication
Business Communication Today! *Thomas & Fryar*
Handbook for Business Writing, *Baugh, Fryar, & Thomas*
Meetings: Rules & Procedures, *Pohl*

Dictionaries
NTC's Classical Dictionary
NTC's Dictionary of Changes in Meaning
NTC's Dictionary of Confusing Words and Meanings
NTC's Dictionary of Literary Terms
NTC's Dictionary of Word Origins
Robin Hymans' Dictionary of Quotations

Essential Skills
Building Real Life English Skills, *Starkey & Penn*
English 93, *Reynolds, Steet, & Guillory*
English Survival Series, *Maggs*
Essential Life Skills
Essentials of English Grammar, *Baugh*
Essentials of Reading and Writing English Series
Grammar for Use, *Hall*
Grammar Step-by-Step, *Pratt*
Guide to Better English Spelling, *Furness*
How to Improve Your Study Skills, *Coman & Heavers*
Reading by Doing, *Simmons & Palmer*
303 Dumb Spelling Mistakes, *Downing*
TIME: We the People, *ed. Schinke-Llano*
Vocabulary by Doing, *Beckert*

Genre Literature
The Detective Story, *Schwartz*
The Short Story & You, *Simmons & Stern*
Sports in Literature, *Emra*
You and Science Fiction, *Hollister*

Journalism
Getting Started in Journalism, *Harkrider*
Journalism Today! *Ferguson & Patten*

Language, Literature, and Composition
An Anthology for Young Writers, *Meredith*
The Art of Composition, *Meredith*
Creative Writing, *Mueller & Reynolds*
Literature by Doing, *Tchudi & Yesner*
Lively Writing, *Schrank*
Look, Think & Write, *Leavitt & Sohn*
Publishing the Literary Magazine, *Klaiman*
The Writer's Handbook, *Karls & Szymanski*
Writing by Doing, *Sohn & Enger*
Writing in Action, *Meredith*

Media Communication
Photography in Focus, *Jacobs & Kokrda*
Television Production Today! *Kirkham*
Understanding Mass Media, *Schrank*
Understanding the Film, *Johnson & Bone*

Mythology
Mythology and You, *Rosenberg & Baker*
Welcome to Ancient Greece, *Millard*
Welcome to Ancient Rome, *Millard*
World Mythology, *Rosenberg*

Speech
The Basics of Speech, *Galvin, Cooper, & Gordon*
Contemporary Speech, *HopKins & Whitaker*
Creative Speaking, *Buys et al.*
Creative Speaking Series
Dynamics of Speech, *Myers & Herndon*
Getting Started in Public Speaking, *Prentice & Payne*
Listening by Doing, *Galvin*
Literature Alive! *Gamble & Gamble*
Person to Person, *Galvin & Book*
Public Speaking Today! *Prentice & Payne*
Speaking by Doing, *Buys, Sills, & Beck*

Theatre
Acting & Directing, *Grandstaff*
The Book of Cuttings for Acting & Directing, *Cassady*
The Book of Scenes for Acting Practice, *Cassady*
The Dynamics of Acting, *Snyder & Drumsta*
An Introduction to Theatre and Drama, *Cassady & Cassady*
Play Production Today! *Beck et al.*
Stagecraft, *Beck*

Career Planning
OPPORTUNITIES IN...
Acting Careers
Advertising Careers
Book Publishing Careers
Broadcasting Careers
Business Communications Careers
Film Careers
Journalism Careers
Magazine Publishing Careers
Public Relations Careers
Teaching Careers
Theatrical Design & Production
Writing Careers

How to Write a Winning Résumé
How to Have a Winning Job Interview

For a current catalog and information about our complete line
of language arts books, write:
National Textbook Company
a division of NTC Publishing Group
4255 West Touhy Avenue
Lincolnwood (Chicago), Illinois 60646-1975 U.S.A.